POST-BIBLICAL
HEBREW LITERATURE

POST-BIBLICAL
HEBREW LITERATURE

AN ANTHOLOGY

★★

English Translation

By

B. HALPER, M. A., Ph. D.
Dropsie College, Philadelphia

Philadelphia
The Jewish Publication Society of America
1921

PREFACE

Although the Hebrew language ceased to be the vernacular of the majority of the Jewish people during the last years of the second temple, it has, throughout the various periods, with but few exceptions, persisted as the medium for the noblest literary productions of the nation. Irrespective of the language spoken by the people in the countries of their adoption, the best thoughts of the Jewish writers found expression in the holy tongue. The Gemara, which is preponderately in Aramaic, can hardly be regarded as an exception, for it consists, in the main, of records of oral discussions and arguments, which were naturally carried on in the vernacular, and as such it is not to be classed among works of literature in its narrower sense. On the other hand, it is very significant that the Midrash and some of the midrashic elements in the Talmud are mostly in Hebrew, and it is just these parts which may claim to be regarded as literature. Then the prayers, many of which date from the early centuries of the present era, and the piyyutim are practically all in Hebrew.

When the centre of Jewish literary activity was transferred to Arabic-speaking countries, the Hebrew language still continued to be employed by a good many of the writers. The treatises with a practical purpose, intended for the edification of the people at large, were, it is true, written in the vernacular, but the literary productions were composed in Hebrew. Lexicographical, grammatical, and philosophical books

5

appealed to the general public, and had therefore to
be expressed in the language spoken by the people.
But Hebrew was employed for the literary compositions, poems, and piyyutim. Sa'adya, Ibn Gebirol,
and Judah ha-Levi wrote their philosophic works,
which undoubtedly had a didactic aim, in Arabic, but
their poems and hymns are invariably in Hebrew.
Moreover, the popularity of books written in Arabic
was short-lived. For shortly afterwards the centre
of Jewish learning was shifted to other countries,
and the vast Jewish-Arabic literature inevitably became
a sealed book. While the Hebrew translations of
Sa'adya's *Faiths and Creeds,* Bahya's *Duties of the
Heart,* Judah ha-Levi's *Khazarite,* and Maimonides'
Guide of the Perplexed have been repeatedly printed,
the Arabic originals of these books had been mould-
ing in the various libraries until scholars in comparatively recent years unearthed them and published them
for the use of the few scientific investigators. A
similar fate has befallen the grammatical treatises of
the brilliant grammarians of the tenth and eleventh
centuries. The works written in Arabic, in spite of
their intrinsic merit, have almost entirely been forgotten, having been superseded by Hebrew manuals
of an inferior character. In this case the Hebrew
translations did not save them from oblivion to which
they have been condemned for centuries. For the
Hebrew writers of the subsequent periods, who knew
Arabic, borrowed from their predecessors, and presented the material in a manner acceptable to their
readers.

The continuity of the Hebrew language as a
literary medium is, accordingly, unbroken, and to illustrate this fact by examples is one of the aims of this

Anthology.   Incidentally a study of the numerous
extracts incorporated into this volume will establish
the truth, which has too often been ignored, that the
Hebrew genius did not become stagnant with the
conclusion of the biblical Canon.   It is true that the
literary quality of post-biblical works cannot approach
the sublimity and beauty of the Bible; but this verdict
may justly be applied to other literatures.   During
the last two thousand years no literature which could
rank with the canonical books of the Bible has been
produced.

Apart from the literary criterion, there is another
aspect which differentiates post-biblical Hebrew
literature from the Bible: the former is the product
of men, who, with the exception of Ben Sira and
possibly the teachers of the Mishnah, did not speak
Hebrew as their mother-tongue.   Their style, as a
consequence, bears the marks of artificiality, and in
many cases lacks spontaneity.   Hebrew was for them
a dead and foreign tongue, and this circumstance
involved numerous obstacles and disadvantages.
Some of the medieval Hebrew poets had to confine
themselves to the vocabulary preserved in the Bible,
and rarely ventured to employ expressions occurring in
the Talmud or to coin new words which were needed
for their poetic compositions.   They were thus denied
that freedom of expression which is essential to the
creative genius, and were compelled to fit their work
to the frame.   It is due to these considerations that
some of the hymns appear like strings of biblical
verses or phrases, more or less skilfully put together.
The original and daring spirits among these writers,
in order to express their new ideas and sentiments,
were driven to invest the biblical words and phrases

with new significations, and thereby developed a novel style, which, though interesting in itself and doing credit to the ingenuity of the authors, could not have been conducive to literary creativeness. For while in quest of a biblical phrase which should serve as a vehicle for his newly-conceived thought, the poet could not give free rein to his fancy. And yet, despite all these disadvantages, we have before us masterly compositions which cannot fail to arouse our interest and admiration. On the other hand, the philosophers, grammarians, lexicographers, historians, and geographers have freely introduced new words and expressions, and have thereby enriched the volume of the Hebrew vocabulary. These new coinages, which, to a great extent, have been sanctioned by the usage of centuries, are of vital interest to us at present owing to the widespread movement to revive the Hebrew language. Instead of beginning with a *tabula rasa,* as is done by some of the leaders of this movement, it would be more advisable, and certainly more scientific, to explore our old treasures. There is ample material in post-biblical Hebrew works for the reconstruction of the language.

This volume of translations is a companion to the Hebrew texts printed in a separate book, and in the case of some extracts the reason for their inclusion in this *Anthology* may not be quite apparent. For, in preparing the selections, I have been guided by two principles: the literary merit of the extract and its pedagogic value. The latter quality would be entirely lost in a translation. A passage whose literary value is not very high, but which is pedagogi- cally important, would naturally be welcomed by the student desirous of familiarizing himself with the style of post-biblical Hebrew. Such a passage, however, may appear cumbersome in translation. At the same time it is hoped that the reader will derive æsthetic pleasure from the beauty or quaintness, as the case may be, of the great variety of passages. In order to give an idea of the diversity and extensiveness of post-biblical Hebrew literature, practically all branches have been incorporated into this *Anthology,* and great care has been taken to select representative authors. Mishnah, Talmud, Midrash, liturgy, poetry, philosophy, ethics, history, geography, folk-lore, travel, philology, epistles, ethical wills, and general compositions are represented in this volume. It is to be regretted that two branches, which have been and are the most potent factors in shaping Jewish intellectual life, could not be included. I refer to Halakah and biblical exegesis, which had to be excluded for the simple reason that the representative passages of these branches scarcely possess literary value. At the same time I have excerpted sections from Maimonides' *Code,* Eleazar of Worms' *Rokeah,* and Abravanel's commentary on the Pentateuch. These extracts, however, do not represent Halakah or exegesis, though they happen to have been incorporated into halakic and exegetical works. For a similar reason Kabbalah is not represented here, although there is a mystical strain in the extract from the *Rokeah* and in Nahmanides' epistle. While in point of time Ben Sira belongs to the biblical period, it has been deemed advisable to incorporate passages from his *Wisdom,* because it is outside the Hebrew Canon. Moreover, in the Hebrew text of the extracts selected for this *Anthology* at least two Hebrew verbs, not occurring in the Bible, have been rescued from oblivion.

The texts are arranged chronologically as far as possible. The method of arranging extracts according to subjects, which other writers may prefer, presents numerous difficulties which are now obviated. Some passages defy classification, while others can be placed in more than one group. Moreover, the chronological arrangement has the advantage of presenting a complete picture of the growth and development of the various branches of Hebrew literature. Although some branches synchronize, as, for instance, poetry and philosophy, few of them persist throughout the various periods. In the majority of cases each age has produced a mode of literary expression peculiar to itself. The eleventh century may be regarded as the Golden Age of Hebrew poetry. A few gifted poets have arisen during the twelfth and thirteenth centuries, but we meet with no great talents until we reach the modern renaissance, the beginnings of which are incorporated here. The philosophic activity extended over a much longer period, but the best works have been produced in a limited number of generations.

The translations are obviously based upon the Hebrew volume of this *Anthology*. A reader comparing my translation with other editions of the extracts will therefore come across some discrepancies. A few examples may suffice to illustrate this point. The printed editions of the Mishnah have a word denoting " silver " which is here rendered by " golden " (II, 2, l. 7). Of course, my edition has the correct word which is found in the famous Munich manuscript. In the Pesikta extract there is an additional sentence not found in any of the editions that have hitherto appeared: *A messenger came and said unto me:*

" *Thy husband died in the city across the sea* " (V, 1,
l. 10). My reading, however, is derived from the
Parma manuscript. In Judah ha-Levi's poem entitled
" Meditations in Mid-Ocean " (XVIII, 2, l. 6 from
end) my translation reads: *The waters and the sky
are like brilliant and bright ornaments on the night.*
The word " ornaments " does not occur in any of the
printed editions, and, instead, they all read two words
which signify " until the sea," which are entirely
unsuitable for the context. My rendering is the result
of a slight emendation involving merely the joining
of the two words into one and a change in the vocalization. In the notes to the Hebrew volume the reader
will find ample justification for the rather numerous
variants. In order not to render this volume cumbersome, those notes have been omitted here.

Wherever possible, I have attempted to retain the
flavor of the original, and the translation is literal
as far as the English idiom would allow. In a number of cases, notably Judah ha-Levi's letter (XVIII, 3),
a free rendering would, I fear, be meaningless. To
my mind, only a literal translation is capable of doing
justice to a literature of this kind. The King James'
Version of the Bible owes part of its charm to its
literalness. Those translators were fortunate in writing during the formative period of the English
language, before the various idioms became fixed
But even in more recent times the superiority of
Burton's *Arabian Nights* must be partly ascribed to
its quaint literalness. This method has been wisely
followed by Chenery and Steingass in translating
Al-Hariri's *Assemblies,* though they lacked Burton's
artistic skill. The average reader is probably not
aware that the literal translator imposes upon himself

a much severer task than the writer who merely gives a free rendering. The former, if he is a conscientious worker, attempts to reproduce everything, while the latter often allows himself to omit or vary difficult expression which task the translator's skill. The unchary reader finds the free translation smooth and easy, and is liable to condemn the literal one, which is necessarily rugged.

Some of the extracts had been previously translated in a satisfactory manner, notably Ben Sira, Kalir, Ibn Gebirol's *Royal Crown,* Benjamin of Tudela, Judah ha-Levi's *Khazarite* (by H. Hirschfeld), and Maimonides' *Guide of the Perplexed* (by M. Friedländer). But in all cases I found it necessary to subject the passages to a thorough revision, partly because my aim was different from that of my predecessors. This revision was especially necessary in the two last-named extracts. Hirschfeld and Friedländer translated the Arabic originals, while I wished to illustrate the style of the Hebrew translators. This fact will also explain another difficulty which may puzzle a reader of this volume: Extracts XXIII and XXVI are listed under Judah b. Saul Ibn Tibbon and Samuel b. Judah Ibn Tibbon, and not under Judah ha-Levi and Moses b. Maimon, respectively. In an anthology of philosophy these sections would naturally be credited to their original authors, but the Hebrew translations must be given under the Ibn Tibbons. And obviously the arrangement of this volume ought to follow that of the Hebrew texts.

Doctor Cyrus Adler has kindly read the manuscript and proof-sheets of this volume, and I am indebted to him for a number of valuable suggestions, especially in connection with the style. My thanks are also due to Professor Israel Davidson and Doctor Isaac Husik for going over the proof-sheets of the poetic and philosophic sections, respectively.

B. HALPER.

DROPSIE COLLEGE, *February, 1920.*

CONTENTS

15

I. THE WISDOM OF BEN SIRA

[This apocryphal book, usually called "Ecclesiasticus," was composed about 180 B. C. E. by Jesus, the son of Simon, the son of Eleazar, the son of Sira. The author was probably a scribe, and was well-versed in the wisdom literature of his day. The Hebrew original of this work was still known in the tenth century, but was subsequently lost sight of. In 1896 a fragment from the Cairo Genizah was given to Prof. S. Schechter, who immediately identified it as the Hebrew original of this book. Other discoveries were afterwards made, and now about two-thirds of the entire work have been recovered.]

1. Wisdom Is a Source of Happiness [1]

Happy is the man that meditateth in wisdom,
And that hath respect unto understanding;
That setteth his heart upon her ways,
And considereth her paths;
Going out after her in search of her,
And spying all her entries;
That prieth through her window,
And hearkeneth at her doors;
That encampeth about her house,
And fixeth his pegs into her wall,
And he pitcheth his tent by her side,
And dwelleth in a goodly dwelling;
And he buildeth his nest on her bough,
And lodgeth among her branches;
And he sheltereth in her shade from the heat,
And dwelleth in her habitations.

For he that feareth the Lord doeth this,
And he that taketh hold of the Law attaineth unto her.

[1] Chapters 14.20-15.8.

19

And she will meet him as a mother,
And receive him as a wife of youth.
And she will feed him with the bread of under-
    standing,
And give him water of knowledge to drink.
And he is stayed upon her, and shall not be moved;
And in her he trusteth, and shall not be confounded.
And she will exalt him above his neighbor,
And in the midst of the congregation will she open
    his mouth.
He shall find joy and gladness,
And she will make him inherit an everlasting name.
Men of vanity shall not attain unto her,
And men of arrogance shall not see her.
Far from scorners is she,
And liars remember her not.

2. The Usefulness of the Physician [2]

Honor a physician according to thy need of him—
Him also hath God apportioned.
From God a physician getteth wisdom,
And from a king he receiveth gifts.
The skill of a physician lifteth up his head,
And he may stand before nobles.
God bringeth out medicines from the earth,
And let a prudent man not despise them.
Was not water made sweet by wood,
To make every man know His power?
And He gave men understanding,
That they might glory in His mighty works.
By means of them doth a physician assuage pain,

[2] Chapter 38, 1-15.

And likewise the apothecary maketh a confection:
That His work may not cease,
Nor health from the sons of men.

My son, in sickness be not negligent;
Pray unto God, for He healeth.
Flee from iniquity, and from respect of persons,
And from all transgressions cleanse thy heart.
Offer a sweet savor as a memorial,
And prepare a fat offering according to thy substance,
And also to the physician give a place,
And he shall not be removed, for there is need of him
    likewise.
For there is a time when in his power is good success,
For he, too, maketh supplication to God,
That He should prosper to him the treatment,
And the healing, for the sake of his living.
He that sinneth against his Maker
Behaveth himself proudly before a physician.

3. In Praise of the High Priest Simeon the Son of Johanan [3]

Great among his brethren, and glory of his people,
Was Simeon the son of Johanan, the priest;
In whose generation the house was repaired,
And in whose days the temple was fortified;
In whose generation a cistern was digged,
A pit like the sea in its abundance;
In whose days a wall was built—
Turrets for protection in the temple of the King:
Who took thought for his people against the spoiler,
And fortified the city against the besieger.

[3] Chapter 50, 1-24.

How glorious was he when he looked forth from the
  Tent,
And when he went out from the sanctuary!
As the morning-star from amid thick clouds,
And as the full moon in the days of the solemn feast;
As the sun dawning upon the temple of the King,
And as a rainbow seen in the cloud.
As a bud in the branches in the days of the solemn
  feast,
And as the lily by the watercourses;
As the flower of Lebanon in the days of summer,
And as the fire of incense upon the meal-offering:
As a gold vessel . . . .[4]
That is set with precious stones;
As a green olive full of berries,
And as a wild olive-tree with branches full of sap.
When he put on robes of honor,
And clothed himself with robes of glory;
When he ascended the altar of majesty,
And made glorious the court of the sanctuary;
When he received the portions from the hand of his
  brethren,
While standing by the altar-fires:
Round him the garland of his sons,
Like cedar-plants in Lebanon.
And they compassed him about like willows of the
  brook—
All the sons of Aaron in their glory;
With the fire-offerings of the Lord in their hand,
Before all the congregation of Israel;
Until he had finished serving the altar,
And arranging the fires of the Most High.

[4] There are some illegible letters in the original.

Then sounded the sons of Aaron, the priests,
With trumpets of beaten work;
And they sounded, and made their mighty voice heard,
To bring to remembrance before the Most High.
All flesh hastened together,
And fell down on their faces to the ground;
Worshipping before the Most High,
Before the Holy One of Israel.
And the choir uttered its voice,
And over the multitude they made sweet melody.
And all the people of the land chanted,
In prayer before the Merciful;
Until he had finished serving the altar,
And had brought his customary offerings unto it.
Then he came down, and lifted up his hands
Over all the congregation of Israel;
And the blessing of the Lord was on his lips,
And in the name of the Lord he gloried.
And they bowed down again a second time,
The people, all of them, before Him.

Now bless ye the Lord, the God of Israel,
Who doeth wondrously on earth;
Who bringeth up man from the womb,
And maketh him according to His will.
May He give you wisdom of heart,
And may He be with peace among you.
May He make His mercy stand fast with Simeon,
And may He confirm to him the covenant of Phinehas,
That shall not be cut off from him and from his seed,
As the days of heaven.

II. THE MISHNAH

[A collection of Jewish jurisprudence, dealing with the various aspects of Jewish life, and classified in the following six orders: *Zera'im* ("Seeds"), containing eleven tractates; *Mo'ed* ("Festivals"), containing twelve tractates; *Nashim* ("Women"), containing seven tractates; *Nezikin* ("Damages"), containing ten tractates; *Kodashim* ("Holy Things"), containing eleven tractates; *Teharot* ("Purifications"), containing twelve tractates. The Mishnah is written in terse and simple Hebrew, well adapted to the various subjects, and has preserved a number of words, which, as may be seen from the cognate languages, must have been in common use in biblical times, though they do not occur in the Bible. It also contains some loan-words from Aramaic, Greek, and Latin. It was redacted by Rabbi Judah ha-Nasi about 200 C. E.]

1. The Bringing of the First-Fruits to Jerusalem [1]

In what manner were the first-fruits brought up? All the inhabitants of the towns of a district assembled in the principal city of the district; they spent the night in the market-place of the city, and entered no house. Early in the morning the appointed officer would proclaim: 'Arise, and let us go up to Zion, to the house of the Lord our God.'

They that lived in the vicinity would bring fresh figs and grapes; they that came from afar would bring dry figs and raisins. The bull went before them, its horns overlaid with gold, and a garland of olive-leaves on its head. The flute played before them, until they drew near Jerusalem. When they drew near Jerusalem, they sent messengers before them, and adorned their first-fruits. The governors, deputies, and treasurers came out to meet them; according to the rank

[1] Tractate Bikkurim 3. 2-8.

24

of those that entered did they come out. All the craftsmen of Jerusalem stood up before them, and greeted them, saying: 'Our brethren, ye men of such and such a place, ye are welcome.'

The flute played before them, until they reached the temple mount. When they reached the temple mount, each man (even king Agrippa) put his basket upon his shoulders. Then they went in as far as the temple court. When they reached the temple court, the Levites recited the song: 'I will extol Thee, O Lord, for Thou hast raised me up, and hast not suffered mine enemies to rejoice over me.'[2]

The pigeons which were fastened to the baskets were offered as sacrifices, while those which they held in their hands were given to the priests.

While the basket was still on his shoulder, he recited from *I profess this day unto the Lord thy God,*[3] till he finished the entire portion. Rabbi Judah says: Only as far as *A wandering Aramean was my father.*[4] When he reached the words *A wandering Aramean was my father,* he took the basket down from his shoulder, held it by its rim (while the priest put his hand under it, and waved it), and recited from *A wandering Aramean was my father,* until he finished the entire portion. He then placed his basket at the side of the altar, prostrated himself, and went out.

Formerly any one who was able to read would read by himself, while he who could not read would repeat after the reader. But as many people refrained from

[2] Psalm 30. 2.
[3] Deuteronomy 26. 3.
[4] *Ibid.* 26. 5.

bringing the first-fruits on account of this, it was in-
stituted that both, those that are able to read and
those that are not able, should repeat after the reader.

The wealthy would bring their first-fruits in baskets
of silver or of gold, while the poor would bring them
in wicker baskets made of peeled willow-twigs. The
baskets and the first-fruits were given to the priests.

2. The Libation of Water and the Water-Drawing Feast [5]

In what manner was the libation of water made?
A golden pitcher of the capacity of three logs was
filled with water from the brook of Shiloah. When
they reached the Water Gate, they sounded a plain
note, a tremolo, and a plain note. The priest went
up the ascent of the altar, and turned to his left,
where stood two golden basins. Rabbi Judah says:
They were of gypsum, but their appearance was darkish
because of the wine. In each was a hole like a narrow nostril, one of the basins having a big opening
and the other a small one, so that both should become
empty at the same time. The basin toward the west
was for water, that toward the east for wine. But
if the water is poured into the basin for wine, or the
wine into the basin for water, it is lawful. Rabbi
Judah says: The libation was performed with one log
during all the eight days. Unto him who poured out
the water they said: ' Raise thy hands; ' because it once
happened that a priest poured the water over his feet,
and all the people pelted him to death with their citrons.

As they did on week-days, so they did on the Sabbath, except that on the eve of the Sabbath they would

[5] Tractate Sukkah 4. 9-5. 4.

fill a golden pitcher, which had not been consecrated, with water from the brook of Shiloah, and place it in the chamber. If the water was spilt, or uncovered, they would fill the pitcher with water from the laver; for wine or water, which was uncovered, is not fit to be offered on the altar.

He who did not see the rejoicing of the water-drawing never saw real rejoicing in his life.

At the expiration of the first day of Tabernacles they[6] descended to the Women's Court, where they made great preparations. Golden candlesticks were there, upon whose tops were four golden basins. Four ladders were placed near each candlestick, and four young priests held pitchers of oil containing one hundred and twenty logs, which they poured into basins.

Of the worn-out breeches and girdles of the priest wicks were made, wherewith to kindle the lamps. There was not a court in Jerusalem which was not illuminated by the lights kindled at the water-drawing.

Pious and distinguished men danced before them with torches in their hands, and chanted before them hymns and praises. The Levites with harps, lutes, cymbals, and trumpets, and musical instruments without number stood upon the fifteen steps, that led from the Men's Court to the Women's Court, corresponding to the fifteen Songs of Ascent of the Book of Psalms. Upon these steps the Levites had stood with musical instruments, and chanted hymns. Two priests with trumpets in their hands stood at the Upper Gate, which led down from the Men's Court to the Women's Court. When the cock crowed, they sounded a plain

[6] That is, the priests and Levites.

note, a tremolo, and a plain note. When they reached
the tenth step, they again sounded a plain note, a
tremolo, and a plain note. When they reached the
Court, they once more sounded a plain note, a tremolo,
and a plain note. They continued to blow the horn,
until they reached the gate that led out to the east.
As soon as they reached the gate that led out to the
east, they turned their faces from east to west, and said:
' Our fathers who were in this place turned their backs
toward the temple and their faces toward the east,
and prostrated themselves eastward to the sun; but
as for us, our eyes are turned to God.' Rabbi Judah
says: They repeated it,' and said: ' We are God's
and our eyes are turned to God.'

' That is, perhaps, they repeated God's name.

III. ABOT DE-RABBI NATHAN

[A sort of Tosefta (addition) to *Pirke Abot* (Saying of the Fathers). It contains homiletic expositions, based upon the mishnic text of that tractate, as well as a number of independent maxims and narratives. It is divided into forty chapters (in some editions there are forty-one), and is of tannaitic origin. Two recensions are extant.]

Rabban Johanan the Son of Zaccai's Pupils Offer Consolations to Their Master on the Death of His Son [1]

When the son of Rabban Johanan the son of Zaccai died, his pupils came to console him. Rabbi Eliezer entered, sat down before him, and said unto him: 'O master, is it thy will that I should say something to thee?' He replied: 'Speak.' Rabbi Eliezer then said unto him: 'Adam had a son who died, and yet he accepted consolation for him. Whence do we know that he accepted consolation for him? because it is written: "And Adam knew his wife again." [2] Accept thou consolation likewise.' Whereupon Rabban Johanan said unto him: 'Is it not enough that I am grieved, must thou also remind me of Adam's grief?' Rabbi Joshua then entered, and said unto him: 'Is it thy will that I should say something to thee?' He replied: 'Speak.' Rabbi Joshua then said unto him: 'Job had sons and daughters all of whom died in one day, and yet he accepted consolation for them. Accept thou consolation likewise. Whence do we know that Job accepted consolation? because it is written:

[1] Chapter 14, Schechter's edition, p. 58.
[2] Genesis 4. 25.

29

" The Lord gave, and the Lord hath taken away;
blessed be the name of the Lord." ' * Whereupon Rabban Johanan said unto him : ' Is it not enough that I am
grieved, must thou also remind me of Job's grief ? '
Rabbi Jose then entered, sat down before him, and
said unto him : ' O master, is it thy will that I should
say something to thee ? ' He replied : ' Speak.' Rabbi
Jose then said unto him : ' Aaron had two grown-up
sons both of whom died in one day, and yet he accepted consolation, as it is written : " And Aaron
held his peace " ; * now silence implies consolation. Accept thou consolation likewise.' Whereupon Rabban
Johanan said unto him : ' Is it not enough that I am
grieved, must thou also remind me of Aaron's grief ? '
Rabbi Simon then entered, and said unto him : ' O
master, is it thy will that I should say something to
thee ? ' He replied : ' Speak.' Rabbi Simon then
said unto him : ' King David had a son who died,
and yet he accepted consolation. Accept thou consolation likewise. Whence do we know that David
accepted consolation ? because it is written : " And
David comforted Bath-sheba his wife, and went in
unto her, and lay with her ; and she bore a son,
and he called his name Solomon." * Accept thou, O
master, consolation likewise.' Whereupon Rabban Johanan said unto him : ' Is it not enough that I am
grieved, must thou also remind me of king David's
grief ? ' Rabbi Eleazar the son of Arak then entered.
As soon as Rabban Johanan saw him, he said unto his
attendant : ' Take his garments, and walk after him into

³ Job 1. 21.
⁴ Leviticus 10. 3.
⁵ 2 Samuel 12. 24.

the bath-house,[6] for he is a great man, and I cannot withstand him!' Rabbi Eleazar entered, sat down before him, and said unto him: ' I shall give thee a parable to which this matter is like: it is like to a man to whom the king committed a trust. Every day that man would weep, and cry, saying: " When shall I be freed of this trust in peace? " Such is thy case, O master: thou hadst a son who studied the Torah, the Pentateuch, Prophets, and Writings, the Mishnah, Halakot, and Haggadot, and departed from this world without sin. Thou shouldst surely accept consolation for him, when thou hast restored thy trust unimpaired.' Whereupon Rabbi Johanan said unto him: ' Eleazar my son, thou hast comforted me in the manner men should comfort.'

When they went forth from his presence, Rabbi Eleazar said: ' I shall go to Dimsith which is a beautiful place with pleasant and delicious waters.' But the others said: ' We shall go to Jamnia, where there are many scholars who love the Torah.' He who went to Dimsith which is a beautiful place with pleasant and delicious waters, his fame as a scholar waned; but they who went to Jamnia, where there are many scholars who love the Torah, their fame as scholars became great.

[6] This is an expression, of frequent occurrence in Aramaic, denoting: *pay him homage*. Comp. 'Erubin 27b.

IV. THE BABYLONIAN TALMUD

[Lengthy discussions of the subjects treated of in the Mishnah. It likewise contains numerous anecdotes and legends. While most of the discussions relate to the legal and ritual topics, the Talmud may at the same time be termed a store-house of almost all the sciences cultivated in those days, as medicine, astronomy, and mathematics. It is of extreme interest to the student of folk-lore. The noblest minds of the Jewish race have up till comparatively recent times been devoted to the study of the volumes of the Talmud, which has contributed to the shaping of the Jewish character. The language is for the most part Aramaic, but Hebrew passages occur now and again. It was redacted about 500 c. E.]

1. The Martyrdom of Rabbi Akiba [1]

Once upon a time the wicked Roman government decreed that the Israelites should not study the Torah. One day Pappos the son of Judah met Rabbi Akiba, who publicly called assemblies together, and studied the Torah. He said: ' Akiba, fearest thou not the government?' Rabbi Akiba replied: 'I shall give thee a parable: A fox walked about by the riverside. Perceiving fishes that were fleeing in companies from place to place, he said unto them: " Why do ye flee?" They answered: " On account of the nets that men bring against us." He said unto them: "Do ye wish to go up to the dry land, so that I and ye may live together in the same manner as my forebears lived with your forebears?" They said unto him: " Art thou he who is said to be the shrewdest of the animals? Thou art not shrewd, but foolish. If we are terror-stricken in the place where we live, how much greater our fear in the place where we are like to die!" This is our case. If we are in such distress now that we study the Torah, concerning

[1] Tractate Berakot 61b.

32

which it is written: " For it is thy life and the length of days; " [2] how much more shall we be in distress, if we cease to study the Torah! '

It is related that before many days passed Rabbi Akiba was seized and put into prison. Pappos likewise was seized and put next to Rabbi Akiba, who said unto him: ' O Pappos, why wast thou brought here?' He replied: ' Happy art thou, Akiba, that thou wast seized because of the words of the Torah; woe unto Pappos who was seized because of vain things.'

Rabbi Akiba was led forth to be put to death at the time for reading the Shema'. While they tore his flesh with iron combs, he took upon himself the yoke of the kingdom of heaven. His pupils asked: ' O master, thus far?' He replied: ' All my life have I been distressed about this verse: " With all thy soul " [3] (even if He takes away thy soul); I used to say: When shall I have the opportunity to fulfil it? Shall I not fulfil it now that the opportunity is come?' He prolonged the word *One,* so that his soul departed while he uttered the word *One.* A heavenly voice came forth, and said: ' Happy art thou, Rabbi Akiba, because thy soul departed at the word *One.*' The ministering angels said unto the Holy One, blessed be He: ' Is this the Torah, and this the reward thereof? *Is Thy hand governed by men, O Lord?* ' [4] He replied unto them: ' *Their portion is in eternal life.*' [5] A heavenly voice came

[2] Deuteronomy 30. 20.
[3] *Ibid.* 6. 5.
[4] Psalm 17. 14. A haggadic interpretation is given here. Rashi offers a different explanation. It is also possible, by changing the vocalization, to translate: *These are slain for Thy hand.*
[5] *Ibid.*

forth, and said: 'Happy art thou, Rabbi Akiba; thou art ready for the life of the world to come.'

2. A Controversy on the Merits of Charity [6]

Turnus Rufus [7] asked Rabbi Akiba: 'If your God loves the poor, why does he not sustain them?' He replied: 'That we may be delivered from the punishment of Gehenna.' Turnus Rufus said: 'That would condemn you to Gehenna. I shall give thee a parable. A king of flesh and blood is wroth against his servant, casts him into a dungeon, and decrees that none shall give him food or drink. A man, however, comes, and gives him food and drink. When the king hears of it, will he not be angry with him? Ye are called servants, as it is written: "For unto Me the children of Israel are servants." [8] Rabbi Akiba replied: 'This is not so; let me give thee a parable. A king of flesh and blood is wroth against his son, casts him into a dungeon, and commands that none shall give him food or drink. A man, however, comes and gives him food and drink. When the king hears of it, will he not send him gifts? We are called children, as it is written: "Ye are the children of the Lord your God." [9] But Turnus Rufus said unto him: 'Ye are called children, and ye are likewise called servants: when ye do God's will, ye are called children; but when ye do not God's will, ye are called servants. At present, however, ye are not doing God's will.' Rabbi Akiba replied: 'Nevertheless it is written: "Is it

[6] Tractate Baba Batra 10a.
[7] A Roman commander in Judea under Hadrian. Turnus stands either for Tyrannus or T. Annius.
[8] Leviticus 25. 55.
[9] Deuteronomy 14. 1.

not to deal thy bread to the hungry, and that thou bring the poor that are cast out to thy house? " [10] Now to which time do the words *bring the poor that are cast out to thy house* apply? Certainly to the present time, and yet it is written: " Is it not to deal thy bread to the hungry! " '

3. Maxims and Admonitions [11]

Rabbi Eleazar ha-Kappar says: Keep away from complaining, lest thou shouldst complain against others, and sin all the more. Love him who reproves thee, that thou mayest add wisdom to thy wisdom; hate him who praises thee, that thy wisdom may not be diminished. Love the synagogue, that thou mayest take thy reward every day; love the house of study, that thy children may be inspired to study the Torah. Love the poor, that thy children may not come to that state. Love humility, that thou mayest complete the years of thy life. Love acts of beneficence, that thou mayest be delivered from the angel of untimely death. Be careful in reading the Shema' and prayers, that thou mayest be delivered from the punishment of Gehenna. Let thy house be open wide, that thou mayest not lack sustenance. Take heed that the doors of thy house should not be locked when thou reclinest at the table to eat and to drink; for the doors of thy house sometimes lead thee to poverty. Take care of the honor of thy wife, that she may not be like a barren woman. Be joyful when thou art afflicted with pain, for this delivers thee from the punishment of

[10] Isaiah 58. 7.
[11] Tractate Derek Erez Zuta, chapter 9, Tawrogi's edition pp. 45, *seq.*

Gehenna. Rejoice in thy table when the hungry derive pleasure from it; for thereby thou wilt prolong thy days in this world and in the world to come. Be joyful when thou hast given away aught from thy house, that the anger of the angel of death may be averted from thee, as it is written: 'A gift in secret pacifieth anger; and a present in the bosom strong wrath.' [12] If thou hast refrained thyself from doing a good deed, the angel of death will meet thee; but if thou hast caused thy feet to hurry for the sake of the poor and for the sake of the commandments, the words *Blessed art thou when thou comest in, and blessed art thou when thou goest out* [13] apply to thee. If thou keepest thy mouth from slander, thou wilt be all thy days in peace. If thou hast been impudent before one who is greater than thou, thou wilt in the end become leprous. If thou hast refrained thyself from a good deed, and has occupied thyself with a sinful deed, thy wife will in the end die of a plague, as it is written: 'Son of man, behold, I take away from thee the desire of thine eyes with a plague.' [14] If thou hast run to honor a sage, thou wilt have sons and daughters who are righteous before Heaven; and if thou hast run to honor a poor man, thou wilt have sons who study the Torah and fulfil the commandments in Israel. If thou seest that a sage has died, turn not away from him until thou hast accompanied him to the grave; so that when thou diest, thou shalt enter into peace and rest in thy bed. If thou seest that thy friend is impoverished, and that his hand has failed, send him not back empty, as it is written: 'Whoso keepeth

[12] Proverbs 21. 14.
[13] Deuteronomy 28. 6.
[14] Ezekiel 24. 16.

the commandment shall know no evil thing.' [15] If
thou hast lent him aught in the hour of his need, the
words *Then shalt thou call, and the Lord will answer* [16]
will apply to thee. If thou hast humbled thyself, the
Holy One, blessed be He, will lift thee up; but if thou
hast made thyself haughty before thy friend, the
Holy One, blessed be He, will humble thee. Pursue
peace, and people shall tell of thy peace as of the peace
of Phinehas the son of Eleazar. And thus did Rabbi
Eleazar say: Love peace, and hate strife. Great is
peace, for even if the Israelites worship idols, but
peace reigns in their midst, the Shekinah, as it were,
can do them no harm, as it is written: ' Ephraim is
united, though he has idols, let him alone.' [17] But if
strife is in their midst, what is written concerning
them? 'Their heart is divided: now shall they be
destroyed.' [18] How does this apply? A house in which
there is strife will in the end be laid waste. The sages
say: A synagogue in which there is strife will in the
end be demolished. If two scholars dwelling in one
city have two courts of justice, and there is strife in
their midst, they will die an untimely death.

Abba Saul says: Strife between courts of justice
brings about the destruction of the world.

[15] Ecclesiastes 8. 5.
[16] Isaiah 58. 9.
[17] Hosea 4. 17. A haggadic interpretation is here given.
[18] *Ibid.* 10. 2.

V. THE MIDRASH

[The midrashic literature is divided into two main classes: halakic and haggadic. The former deals with legal matters, while the latter, which comprises the greater part of midrashic collections, is exegetic and homiletic. Some of the books are arranged in accordance with the order of the biblical passages upon which they are based, while others are groups of homilies delivered on the important Sabbaths and festivals. The language of this branch of literature is mostly Hebrew, and is very fluent and sometimes poetic, but Aramaic passages occur now and then, especially in the older collections. These works were compiled and redacted at various times, from the tannaitic period down to the twelfth century, and are mostly of Palestinian origin.]

1. The Prophet Jeremiah Meets Mother Zion Mourning for Her Exiled Children [1]

Jeremiah said: While going up to Jerusalem, I lifted up mine eyes, and saw a woman sitting on the top of a mountain, clad in black garments, her hair dishevelled; she was crying and asking who would comfort her, and I was crying and asking who would comfort me. I drew nigh unto her, and said: 'If thou art a woman, speak to me; if thou art a ghost, depart from me.' She replied: 'Dost thou not know me? I am she who had seven children; their father went away to a city across the sea. A messenger came and said unto me: "Thy husband died in the city across the sea." While I went about weeping for him, another messenger came, and said unto me: "The house fell upon thy seven children, and killed them." Now I know not for whom I should weep and for whom I should dishevel my hair.' I said: 'Thou

[1] Pesikta Rabbati, Friedmann's edition, p. 131b.

38

art not better than my mother Zion, and yet she
has become pasture for the beasts of the field.' She
answered and said unto me: ' I am thy mother Zion,
I am the mother of the seven, for thus it is written:
" She that hath borne seven languisheth." ' [2] Jeremiah then said unto her: ' Thy misfortune is like
the misfortune of Job: Job's sons and daughters
were taken away from him, and likewise thy sons and
daughters were taken away from thee; I [3] took away
from Job his silver and gold, and from thee, too, did I
take away thy silver and gold; I cast Job on the
dunghill, and likewise thee did I make into a dunghill.
And just as I returned and comforted Job, so shall
I return and comfort thee; I doubled Job's sons and
daughters, and thy sons and daughters shall I also
double; I doubled Job's silver and gold, and unto thee
I shall do likewise; I shook Job from the dunghill, and
likewise concerning thee it is written: " Shake thyself from the dust; arise, and sit down, O Jerusalem." [4]
A mortal of flesh and blood built thee, a mortal of
flesh and blood laid thee waste; but in the future I
shall build thee, for thus it is written: " The Lord
doth build up Jerusalem, He gathereth together the
dispersed of Israel." ' [5]

2. The Death of Moses [6]

The Holy One said to Gabriel: ' O Gabriel, Go, and
bring Me the soul of Moses.' But he replied: ' Lord of

[2] Jeremiah 15. 9.
[3] Here and in the following sentences the prophet speaks for
God.
[4] Isaiah 52. 2.
[5] Psalm 147. 2.
[6] This narrative is part of a Midrash especially devoted to
this subject, entitled *Midrash Petirat Mosheh,* which was
added at the end of Debarim Rabbah.

the universe, how can I look upon the death of him who
is equal to the sixty myriads of Israel? How can I cause
anguish to such a man?' God then said to Michael:
'Go, and bring Me the soul of Moses.' He replied:
'Lord of the universe, I was his teacher, and he was
my pupil; I cannot look upon his death.' Whereupon
God said to Sammael the wicked: 'Go, and bring Me
the soul of Moses.' He immediately clothed himself
with wrath, girded on his sword, wrapped himself in
cruelty, and went to meet Moses. When Sammael
perceived that Moses was sitting and writing the Ineffable Name, that the radiance of his countenance
was like the sun's, and that he resembled an angel of
the Lord of hosts, he was afraid of him, and said:
'It is certain that the angels are not able to take the
soul of Moses.'

Before Sammael appeared, Moses knew that Sammael was coming. As soon as Sammael saw Moses,
trembling with pain, as of a woman in travail, took
hold of him. Sammael could not open his mouth,
until Moses said to him: 'There is no peace, saith the
Lord concerning the wicked!' What art thou doing
here?' He replied: 'I came to take thy soul.'
'Who sent thee?' asked Moses. 'He that created
all creatures,' answered Sammael. 'Thou shalt not
take my soul,' said Moses. 'The souls of all that
enter this world are delivered into my hands,' said
Sammael. 'I am stronger than all who enter this
world,' asserted Moses. 'Wherein lies thy strength?'
asked Sammael. 'I am Amram's son, who came
forth circumcised from my mother's womb, so that
there was no need to circumcise me. On the very day
of my birth I was able to talk; I walked about, and

' Isaiah 48. 22.

spoke to my father and mother; I did not even drink
milk. When I was three months old, I prophesied
and said that I was destined to receive the Torah from
the midst of flames of fire. While walking about in
the streets, I entered the king's palace, and took off
his crown from his head. When eighty years old I
did signs and wonders in Egypt, and brought forth
the sixty myriads of Israel in the sight of all the
Egyptians; I divided the sea into twelve parts, and
made the waters of Marah sweet. I ascended to
heaven, where I walked about, and took part in the
controversy of the angels; I received the Torah of
fire, dwelt under the throne of fire, took shelter
under a pillar of fire, and spoke face to face with God.
I conquered the dwellers of heaven, and revealed their
secrets to the sons of men. I received the Torah from
the right hand of God, blessed be He, and taught it to
Israel. I waged war against Sihon and Og, the two
mightiest men of the Gentiles, who were so tall that
during the flood the waters reached not their ankles.
I made the sun and moon stand still in the height of
the universe, and smote these mighty men with the
staff that was in my hand, and slew them. Who is
there among them that enter this world who can do
all this? Get thee hence, O wicked one; thou must
not stand here; go, and flee from me. I will not give
thee my soul.'

Sammael forthwith returned, and brought word
back to God. But the Holy One said to Sammael:
'Go, and bring the soul of Moses.' He immediately
drew his sword from its sheath, and stood near Moses.
Whereupon Moses grew wroth, seized in his hand the
staff, upon which was engraved the Ineffable Name,

and fell upon him with the Ineffable Name, and taking
a ray of splendor from between his eyes, he blinded
Sammael's eyes. Thus far Moses prevailed.

At the last moment a heavenly voice came forth,
and said: ' The hour of thy death has come.' Moses
then said to the Holy One, blessed be He: ' O Lord
of the universe, remember the day on which Thou
didst reveal Thyself unto me in the bush, and didst
say unto me: "Come, and I will send thee unto
Pharoah, that thou mayest bring forth My people
the children of Israel out of Egypt." [8] Remember the
time when I stood upon mount Sinai for forty days
and forty nights. I implore Thee, deliver me not unto
the hand of the angel of death.' Whereupon a
heavenly voice came forth, and said unto him:
' Fear not! I Myself shall take charge of thee and
of thy burial.'

At that moment Moses arose, and sanctified himself,
as do the Seraphim. The Holy One came down from
the highest heaven of heavens to take the soul of
Moses, and with Him were three ministering angels,
Michael, Gabriel, and Zagzagel. Michael arranged
Moses' bed, and Gabriel spread a garment of fine
linen at his head; Zagzagel was at his feet. Michael
stood at one side, and Gabriel at the other. The Holy
One then said to Moses: ' Moses, close thine eyelids, one upon the other; place thy hands upon thy
breast; place thy feet one upon the other.' Moses did
as he was commanded. At that moment the Holy One
summoned the soul from Moses' body, and said unto
her: ' My daughter, one hundred and twenty years
have I appointed for thee to be in Moses' body; the

[8] Exodus 3. 10.

time to depart has now arrived. Come thou forth,
tarry not.' The soul said unto Him: 'Lord of the
universe, I know that Thou art the God of all spirits,
and that all the souls, the souls of the living and of
the dead, are delivered into Thy hands, and that Thou
didst create and fashion me, and put me into Moses'
body for one hundred and twenty years. Now is
there in the world a body purer than that of Moses,
upon which there never was any pollution, nor worm
and maggot? Therefore I love it, and desire not to depart from it.' But the Holy One said: 'O soul, come
forth, tarry not. I shall bring thee up to the highest
heaven of heavens, and cause thee to dwell under My
Throne of Glory near the Cherubim, Seraphim, and
hosts of other angels.' The soul then said: 'O Lord of
the universe, when from Thy Shekinah in heaven there
came down two angels, Uzzah and Azzael, they coveted
the daughters of the earth, and corrupted their way
upon the earth, so that Thou didst suspend them between heaven and earth. But the son of Amram
has not come in unto his wife from the day Thou
didst reveal Thyself unto him in the bush, as it is
written: "And Miriam and Aaron spoke against
Moses because of the Cushite woman whom he had
married, for he had married a Cushite woman."[9] I
implore Thee, let me remain in Moses' body.'

At that moment the Holy One kissed him, and
took away his soul with a kiss. God wept, and cried,
as it were: 'Who will rise up for Me against the
evil-doers? who will stand up for Me against the
workers of iniquity?'[10] The Holy Spirit said: 'And
there hath not arisen a prophet since in Israel like

[9] Numbers 12. 1.
[10] Psalm 94. 16.

unto Moses.' [11]   The heavens wept, and said: ' And
the upright among men is no more.' [12]   When Joshua
sought his master and found him not, he wept, and
said: ' Help, O Lord, for the godly man hath ceased;
for faithfulness hath failed from the children of men.' [13]
The ministering angels said: ' He executed the
righteousness of the Lord.' [14]   Israel said: ' And His
ordinances with Israel.' [15]   All of them together said:
' He entereth into peace, they rest in their beds, each
one that walketh in his uprightness.' [16]

The memory of the righteous is blessed, and his
soul shall be in the life of the world to come.

[11] Deuteronomy 34. 10.
[12] Micah 7. 2.
[13] Psalm 12. 2.
[14] Deuteronomy 33. 21.
[15] *Ibid.*
[16] Isaiah 57. 2.

VI. ELEAZAR BE-RABBI KALIR

[Opinions differ as to the time and birthplace of this liturgic poet. The latest researches, however, tend to prove that he flourished in Palestine toward the end of the seventh century. He was a very prolific poet, about two hundred of his poems being still extant in the various Mahzorim. His muse is doleful, bewailing the misfortunes of the Jewish people. His style, though chiefly biblical in construction, teems with newly-coined words.]

1. A Complaint [1]

'Why is the glory of kingdoms cast down and still without dominion?' 'Bel she set up as king, and walked after him, against the law of God. Over her was then set the mistress of kingdoms,[2] until God's rule shines forth.'

She burned my dwelling-place, and crushed my saints, and yet her kingdom was prolonged. She spreads on all sides, she bends her bow against me, and extends her yoke. She terrified and crushed the tender people; and yet she still holds sway. She laid bare and waste my temple's foundation; her guile is very deep. She lifted up her head, and took crafty counsel; her hands are exalted. Her cunning burns

[1] This poem, which is found in the Ashkenazic ritual for New Year, consists of fifteen stanzas, and is an acrostic bearing the author's name. Each stanza has three short rhyming lines. The poet asks why the Jewish kingdom is cast down (stanza 1). A brief answer is given by the Holy Spirit (stanzas 2 and 3). The remaining stanzas are uttered by the Jewish nation complaining of the evil done to her by her enemies who as yet have not been punished for their wickedness.

[2] That is, Rome.

in her, she soars to the sky, and is girt with sovereignty. She rent my curtains, and destroyed my tent;
she harrowed and ploughed my land. She props herself with dominion, is girt with sovereignty, and me she
harasses. She plans rebellion, and hastes to serve
strange gods;—God's kingdom she profanes. She
tortures the King's sons, and says before the King:
' Who in heaven is king over me? '

She vaunts against the King's throne: ' There is
no king save me, none else besides me reigns.'

O highest King, reject Thou her from sovereignty;—
restore Thy dominion to Thyself.

2. The Patriarchs and Matriarchs Intercede on Behalf of Their Exiled Children [3]

Jeremiah went about by the fathers' graves, and
said: ' Beloved ones, how can ye lie at rest, while
your children are banished, pierced through with the
sword? Where is then your merit in a land laid
waste? ' The patriarchs all cried with bitter lamen-
tations, because they were bereft of their children;
with an imploring voice they moaned to the Dweller
of the skies: ' Where is Thy pledge: " But I will
for their sakes remember the covenant of their ancestors "? ' [4]

' They changed My glory for vanity; they had no
dread of Me, they feared Me not; when I hid My
face from them, they longed not, and waited not

[3] This poem is found in the Ashkenazic ritual for the Ninth
of Ab. It consists of eleven stanzas of five rhyming lines,
except the last which has four lines. The stanzas are in
alphabetic order, two letters being disposed of in each stanza.
[4] Leviticus 26. 45.

for Me. How shall I then refrain Me when they say: "He is not our God"?'[5]

The father of the multitude[6] cried in their behalf, and implored the Most High God: 'In vain was I tried ten times for their sake, since I now behold their destruction. Where is Thy promise: "Fear not, Abram"?'[7]

'Ah, they have erred and gone astray from Me, and consecrated themselves to strange gods; they counselled to hew out cisterns for them—but broken cisterns are theirs. How shall I refrain Me, when they break the ten commandments?'

And thus cried Isaac wofully unto the Dweller of the skies: 'In vain was I appointed to be slain, since my seed is crushed and ruined. Where is Thy pledge: "But I will establish My covenant with Isaac"?'[8]

'They rebelled against the prophet Jeremiah, and defiled mount Moriah; I am weary of hearing the complaint which rises to Me from the earth. And how shall I refrain Me since Zechariah is slain?'

And then spoke he who was born for study,[9] like jackals shedding tears: 'My little ones whom I reared with care, why did they fly away so soon? Why was I punished a thousandfold for my blood-guilt?'

Then spoke the faithful shepherd,[10] covered with ashes, wallowing in dust: 'The flocks that were entrusted to my care, why were they cut off before their

[5] Jeremiah 5. 12.
[6] That is, Abraham.
[7] Genesis 15. 1.
[8] *Ibid.* 17. 21.
[9] That is, Jacob.
[10] That is, Moses.

time?   Where is Thy pledge: "They shall not
be widowed " ? ' ¹¹

The wailing voice of Leah, tabering upon her breasts,
was then heard; her sister Rachel, too, bemoaned her
sons; Zilpah struck her face; Bilhah lamented, lifting
up her hands.

' Return, O perfect ones, unto your rest; I will fulfil all your desires.   For your sakes was I sent to
Babylon;—I will return your children's captivity.'

¹¹ Jeremiah 51. **5.**

VII. ELDAD HA-DANI.

[A traveller who flourished in the ninth century. According to his narrative, he was a native of East Africa. He seems to have travelled in Spain and Babylon.]

Eldad Leaves His Native Place Beyond the Rivers of Cush [1]

And in this manner did I go forth from beyond the rivers of Cush: I and a Jew of the tribe of Asher boarded a small ship to trade with the sailors. And it came to pass at midnight that the Lord caused a very great and strong wind to blow, so that the ship was wrecked. And the Lord ordained that I should seize hold upon a plank. And when my companion saw this, he likewise seized hold upon that plank with me. And we went up and down with it, until the sea cast us forth amidst a people whose name is Romaranus. They are black Cushites of tall stature, without clothes and without raiment; for they are like animals, and eat men.

When we came to their country, they seized hold upon us. Seeing that my companion was corpulent, plump, and fat, they slew him and devoured him, while he shouted: ' Woe is me, that I should know this people, that the Cushites should eat my flesh.' But me they cast aside, for I had been sick on the ship; and they put me in chains, till I should grow fat and plump. They brought me delicious dishes of for-

[1] Epstein's edition, pp. 23, *seq.*

bidden food; but I ate nothing, and hid the food.
When they asked me whether I ate, I replied: 'Yes,
I ate.'

I stayed with them a long time, till God, blessed
be He, performed a miracle for me, and there came
upon them a big army from another place, who took
them captive, and plundered them, and slew some of
them. And these took me with them among the captives. Those wicked people were fire-worshippers;
every morning they would build a great fire, to which
they would bow and prostrate themselves. I dwelt
with them four years, until they brought me one day
to the city of Azin.

A Jewish merchant of the tribe of Issachar met
me, and bought me for thirty-two pieces of gold,
and returned with me to his country. They inhabit
the mountains of the sea-coast, and are under the
rule of Media and Persia. And they fulfil this verse:
'This book of the Law shall not depart out of thy
mouth.' [2] They have no yoke of the kingdom, but
only the yoke of the Law. They have among them
captains of hosts, but they do not contend with any man
except about the Law. They live in prosperity and
ease; there is no adversary, nor evil occurrence. They
occupy an area of ten days' journey by ten days'
journey, and have abundant cattle and camels and
asses and servants; but they do not rear horses. They
have no weapons, except a knife for killing animals.
There is no extortion, nor robbery among them; even
if they find garments or money on the road, they do
not stretch forth their hands to take them. But there
live near them wicked people, fire-worshippers, who

[2] Joshua 1. 8.

take their mothers and sisters for wives. These, however, neither harm them, nor benefit them. They have a judge; when I asked about him, they told me that his name was Nahshon. The four modes of executing criminals are practised by them. They speak in the holy tongue and in the Persian tongue.

The children of Zebulun inhabit the mountains of Paran, and are on the border of Issachar. And they make tents of hairy skins which are brought to them from Armenia. They reach as far as the river Euphrates, and engage in commerce. The four modes of executing criminals are practised by them in a fitting manner.

The tribe of Reuben dwell opposite to them, behind mount Paran. They live in peace, love, brotherhood, and friendship. They go together to battle, and attack wayfarers; and they divide the booty among them. They walk in the way of the kings of Media and Persia, and speak in the holy tongue and in the Persian tongue. They possess the Bible, Mishnah, Talmud, and Haggadah. Every Sabbath they expound the reasons for the commandments in the holy tongue, and the explanations are given in the Persian tongue.

The tribe of Ephraim and the half-tribe of Manasseh dwell there, in the mountains of Nejd, the city of Mecca, where is the idolatry of Ishmaelites. These are of abhorred soul and cruel heart; they possess horses, and attack wayfarers, and do not spare their enemies. They have nothing but booty to live upon. They are great warriors; one of them vanquishes a thousand.

The tribe of Simeon and the other half-tribe of Manasseh dwell in the land of the Chaldeans, six

months' journey from the temple. They are more
numerous than all the others, and collect tribute from
twenty-five kingdoms; some of the Ishmaelites pay
them tribute.

We in our country say that we have a tradition that
ye, children of the exile, are of the tribes of Judah
and Benjamin, living under the rule of the adherents
of the idolatrous religion, in the unclean land, scattered
among the Romans, who destroyed the house of our
God, and among the Greeks and Ishmaelites. May
their sword enter into their own heart, and may their
bows be broken!

We also have a tradition, handed down from man to
man, that we are the children of Dan. At first we were
in the land of Israel, dwelling in tents. And there were
not among all the tribes of Israel brave warriors like
us. When Jeroboam the son of Nebat, who caused
Israel to sin, and made two golden calves, rebelled, so
that the kingdom of the house of David was divided,
the tribes assembled together, and said: ' Arise, and
make war against Rehoboam and against Jerusalem.'
But the children of Dan replied: ' Why should we fight
against our brethren and against the son of our lord,
David, king of Israel and Judah? Far be it, far be
it from us!' At that time the elders of Israel said:
' There are no mighty men among all the tribes of
Israel like the tribe of Dan.' Whereupon they said to
the children of Dan: ' Arise, and make battle against
the children of Judah.' But they replied: ' By the life
of the head of Dan our father, we shall not make war
with our brethren, and we shall not shed their blood.'

Whereupon the children of Dan took their swords
and spears and bows, and prepared themselves to de-

part from the land of Israel; for we saw that it was
not possible to remain there. They said: 'Let us go
now, and find a resting-place; for if we wait till the
end, they will destroy us.' We took counsel, and determined to go to Egypt to lay it waste, and to destroy
all its inhabitants. But our princes said to us: 'Is
it not written: "Ye shall see them again no more
for ever?"[3] How then can ye prosper?' Then they
said: 'Let us go against Amalek, or against Edom,
or against Ammon and Moab, to destroy them, that
we may dwell in their place.' But our princes replied:
'It is written in the Torah that the Holy One re-
strained the Israelites from passing through their
border.'[4]

Finally they took counsel to go to Egypt, but not
by the way our fathers had gone, nor to lay it waste,
but in order to pass to the river Pishon, to the land of
Cush.

And it came to pass, when we drew near to Egypt,
that trembling seized hold upon the Egyptians. And
they sent word to us: 'Are ye for war or for peace?'
We replied: 'For peace: we shall pass through your
land to the river Pishon, for there we shall find a resting-place.' And it came to pass, because they did not
believe us, that all the Egyptians stood on their watch
until we had passed through their land and reached
the land of Cush, which we found to be a good and
fertile land, having fields, vineyards, gardens, and
parks. The inhabitants of Cush did not prevent the
children of Dan from dwelling with them, for we took
the land by force. And it came to pass, because we

[3] Exodus 14. 13.
[4] Comp. Deuteronomy 2. 4, 9, 19.

wanted to slay all of them, that they became tribu-
taries, paying taxes to the Israelites.   And we dwelt
with them many years, until we were fruitful, and
multiplied exceedingly.   And we had great wealth.

VIII. JOSIPPON

[A historical book written in biblical style. Although
ascribed to the famous historian Josephus, it is a production
of the ninth century at the earliest.]

Mattathias Charges His Sons Before His Death, and Appoints Judah Who Is Called Maccabæus as Leader in His Stead [1]

Now the days of Mattathias drew nigh that he
should die; and he called unto his five sons, and he
encouraged them, and he strengthened them with his
words. And he said unto them: ' My sons, I know
that now many wars will be waged among you, because we arose, and bestirred ourselves to fight for
our people and for our remnant that escaped, and for
the cities of our God. And now, my sons, be jealous
for the sake of your God and for the sake of his
sanctuary; and fear not death, for if ye die in the
battle of the Lord, ye will receive your reward, and
ye will be in the land of the living with our fathers.
Moreover, ye will also inherit a portion and an inheritance in the lot of their inheritance; for all our fathers
were jealous for the Lord, and our God gave them
grace and honor. Know ye not that Phinehas
our father, because he was jealous for the God of
Israel, when he slew Zimri with the Midianitish
woman, received a covenant of salt for ever? And his
priesthood was unto him, and unto his seed after him,
an everlasting covenant; because he was jealous for
his God, and made atonement for the children of
Israel. And the Lord our God therefore raised him

[1] Part of Book IV, chapter 20.

above all the sons of Aaron, our first father, and He gave him His covenant of peace. Also unto all our fathers who were jealous for our God did our God give their reward; and they found favor in the sight of God. Now, my sons, be strong and of good courage, fear not, and be not dismayed on account of these unclean nations; for they trust in their strength that perisheth and in their might that cometh to an end, but ye trust in the strength of the Lord our God which perisheth not and in the power of His might which cometh not to an end. For they trust in the multitude of their troops and in their army, but ye trust in the Lord with whom are strength and power to save by many or by few. And the power of the horse is a vain thing for deliverance, for deliverance is the Lord's. Assemble yourselves, my sons, and be like one man and of one heart; and be jealous for the God of Israel, as your pious fathers were; and the Lord, the God of your strength, will put the dread of you and the fear of you upon your enemies.'

And he called unto Simon his eldest son, and charged him, and said unto him: ' My son, I know that the Lord has put wisdom and understanding in thy heart. And now give, in perfect good will, thy counsel unto thyself and unto the holy people, and withhold not, I pray thee, thyself nor thy counsel from this people. And thou shalt be a father to thy brethren, and they will hearken unto thee in every matter; for the Lord our God has put in thee counsel, and wisdom, and strength.'

And Mattathias said again: ' Call to me Judah my son.' And he was called unto him; and he stood before him. And he said unto him: ' My son Judah, whose

name is called Maccabee, because of thy strength,
hearken to my counsel, so that withersoever thou turnest, thou mayest have good success, and mayest be
prosperous. I know that thou art a man of war, and
that God has put in thee power and strength, so
that thy heart is as the heart of a lion, which melteth
not and feareth not. And now honor the Lord with
thy strength which He has given thee, for everything
is from Him; and go, and fight His battles without
slothfulness; and be not slothful to go to every side,
and to every corner, in the east, and in the west, and
in the north, and in the south, in the holy land, to take
vengeance from the nations who defile it. And be
thou unto the holy people captain of the host and
war Messiah.' [2]

And Judah answered his father, and said: ' Behold,
my lord my father, I will do according to all which thou
hast commanded me.'

And he commanded, and they brought unto him the
vial of oil; and he poured it upon his head, and he
anointed him leader and war Messiah. And all
the people shouted with a great shout, and blew the
trumpet, and they said: ' Long live the leader,' and:
' Long live the anointed.'

And it came to pass, when Mattathias the priest
finished charging his sons, that he expired and died,
and was gathered unto his people. And Judah his son,
who was called Maccabee because of his strength,
arose in his stead from among his sons, to be leader
and anointed. And his brethren and all his father's
house and all the congregation of the pious helped

[2] In Yoma 72b and Horayot 12a this term refers to the
priest who is anointed to encourage the army. Comp. Deuteronomy 20. 2-4.

him.   And he buried his father with great honor.
And after that Judah put on a coat of mail as a mighty
man ; and he girded his armor upon his loins ; and he
went down to the uncircumcised, who were encamped
round the mountain, which they came to take.   And he
smote among them eight thousand and two hundred of
their mighty men.   And he judged Israel with his
sword ; and he purged out the violent from them, and
he destroyed them.   And he trod down to the earth the
strangers that were in all the borders of Israel.   And
the wicked were discomfited through their dread of
him, and the wrong-doers were dismayed through their
fear of him.   And it was that, when he shouted, his
voice was as the voice of the roaring of a lion on the
day he roars to tear the prey.   And all Israel rejoiced
in his deeds, and exulted in his work.   And all the
world was terrified because of his fame.   Then were
kings, greater and mightier than he, dismayed ; and
trembling seized hold upon the chiefs of the earth and
the kings thereof.   And his name went forth among
the nations to the end of all the earth ; and the tales
of the wonders of his war and the terrors of his
mighty deeds reached to the end of the earth.   And
when he was gathered unto his people, all the seed of
Israel praised him, and honored him.   And they
spoke, saying : ' May the spirit of the Lord cause him
to rest, and may he dwell in the secret place of the
Most High, and abide under the shadow of the Almighty, under the tree of life.'

And he went from city to city, and slew all the
wicked of the people of Judah, who were destroying
the people of Israel.

IX. SA'ADYA GAON B. JOSEPH

[This great Gaon was born at Fayyum, Egypt, in 892. He settled in Babylon, and, though a foreigner, was appointed Gaon of Sura. His many-sided activities and achievements are astounding in their magnitude. He discharged his duties as Gaon with stupendous energy, and found time to write numerous books on grammar, lexicography, exegesis, philosophy, Halakah, and liturgy. He excelled in almost all branches, as may be readily seen from his works that are still extant. His greatest achievement was in the domain of biblical philology. Most of his works were written in Arabic, but he was also a master of Hebrew style. He carried on an effective campaign against the Karaites and other sectarians. He died 942.]

A Prayer Entitled *Magen U-Mehayyeh* (Shield and Quickener) [1]

He remembers the lovingkindnesses of the fathers, and answers the children in the time of their distress, because of His name which is called upon them, and because of the merit of their fathers, as He has done from the days of old, and wrought for them this work; as it is written: ' And the Lord was gracious unto them. . . . ' [2] We therefore ask of Thee, O Lord our God, these three things: to be gracious unto us, to have mercy upon us, and to turn unto us. I beseech Thee, O Lord, be gracious unto us by accepting our prayer; as it is written: ' Behold, as the eyes of servants, ...' [3]

I beseech Thee, O Lord, be gracious unto us by accepting our repentance, and by pardoning us; as it is

---

[1] From a manuscript in the library of the Dropsie College.
[2] 2 Kings 13. 23.
[3] Psalm 123. 2.

59

written: 'Therefore thus saith the Lord God: Now
will I bring back the captivity of Jacob, and have
compassion upon the whole house of Israel; and I will
be jealous for My holy name.'[4]   I beseech Thee, O
Lord, turn unto us, and fulfil our request for life;
as it is written: 'And I will have respect unto you,
and make you fruitful. . . . .'[5] For Thy covenant
stands fast forever, and Thy faithfulness is as the
days of heaven, and Thy righteousness shall be forever, and Thy salvation unto all generations. O King
that art a Savior and a Shield: Blessed art thou, O
Lord, Shield of Abraham.

Thou art on high for ever, O Lord, mighty from
eternity to eternity; from everlasting to everlasting
Thou art God. Thy lovingkindness is in the heavens,
and Thy faithfulness reaches unto the skies. Thou
makest Thy might known to the sons of men, and
Thy excellence is over Israel. From the uttermost
part of the earth are Thy songs, and all the ends of the
earth are filled with Thy praise. Thou art the life of
all eternal life, and the life of all the living comes
from before Thee. Thou fashionest them all with the
four kinds of life, which Thou establishest in them
to keep them alive.[6] At first with the spirit of light,
for the light of the spirit completes their soul. The
foundations of the world which Thou hast stretched
forth may be searched out, but Thy praise shall not
depart; for the mountains may depart, but Thy kingdom shall not vanish; the hills may be removed, but

---

[4] Ezekiel 39. 25.
[5] Leviticus 26. 9.
[6] This is the end of a leaf in the manuscript of the original,
and there is a likelihood that some leaves are missing here,
so that the following sentences are not a continuation of this
part.

Thy mercies shall not fail. Man is too brutish to know Thy creatures; man is put to shame, and fathoms not the mystery of Thy beings. The wise are too foolish to speak of Thy might, and as for them who enumerate Thy works, their tongue stammers. The singers find no strength, and as for the minstrels after them, there is no speech in their lips. Even the holy Living Creatures cannot declare all Thy glory, and even the ministering angels cannot tell all Thy praises. Above all songs and hymns art Thou glorified with Thy praises, lauded with Thy hymns, exalted for Thy favors, sanctified in Thy congregations, sung among Thy hosts, glorified for Thy miracles, crowned for Thy might, declared powerful in Thy books, extolled for Thy victories, proclaimed King for Thy dominion, beloved for Thy teachings, honored for Thy attributes, respected for Thy unity, set on high for Thy purity, prayers are offered to Thee for Thy strength, Thy melodies are chanted to Thee; Thou art met in Thy meeting-places, declared majestic for Thy splendor, sought for Thy words, magnified for Thy might, blessed for Thy blessings, declared strong because of all the things Thou didst create in Thy universe: Because of the sun when it rises and when it sets; because of the moon when it stands in the midst of the heaven; because of the stars when they shoot their arrows on the earth, and when they grow dark and withdraw their shining; because of the heavens which are sometimes bright, while at other times they become gloomy and clothe themselves with darkness; because of the lightnings when they dart forth; because of the arrows when they go abroad; because of the whirlwind when it blows; because of the storm

when it rages; because of the clouds when they pour
out water, and the skies when they give forth a sound;
because of the rain when it comes down in abundance;
because of the flood of mighty waters that sweeps over
the earth; because of the earth when it puts forth
grass; because of the fruit-tree when it brings forth
its fruit; because of life when it is fashioned, brought
to the birth and produced; because of the strength of
the young men and the splendor of the old men; because of the day when it gives us light; because of
the night when it grows dark for us; because of the
months when they are renewed; because of the years
when they are changed; because of the kingdoms of
the earth to which Thou givest dominion (Thou shalt
also cause them to pass away, and raise others in their
stead); because of Thy people Israel whom Thou
didst chastise in judgment (Thou shalt also bring
them back, and restore their pristine glory to them).
Above all hymns and praises shall Thy name be sanctified, O God, that art mighty and strong; purified and
blessed; exalted and great; Thou art a distinguished
Judge, Thou art declared majestic, and all meditate
in Thee; Thou are eternal and faithful; Thou art pure
and sustainest all; Thou art pious and wise, good and
pure; Thou art the only One and art upright, powerful and perfect; clothing and capturing; O exalted
King, that art strong and trusted, enduring and for-
giving, mighty and most high, redeeming and deliver-
ing, watchful and righteous, holy and jealous, lofty
and compassionate, Lord and Keeper, perfect and
mighty. He is mentioned on the earth, and it quakes;
on the lightnings, and they run; on the burning coals,
and they are extinguished; on the pestilence, and it

rages ; on the mountains, and they are rent ; on the child, and it goes forth ; on the tempests, and they subside ; on the woman with child, and she brings forth ; on the diseased, and he is healed ; on the sea, and it was divided ; on the chain, and it is loosened ; on the lion, and he turns back ; on the water, and it stands still ; on the river, and it turns back ; on Satan, and he is stupe-fied ; on the world, and it exists ; on the afflicted, and he is cured ; on the rock, and it brings forth water ; on the eloquent, and he becomes silent ; on the thunder, and it ceases ; on the adamant, and it breaks in pieces ; on the depth, and it overflows. All this is be-cause of the glory of Thy name. For as Thy name so is Thy praise, and in Thy name do Thy people exult, and for Thy name's sake dost Thou defer Thine anger, and givest glory to Thy name. For whosoever knows Thy name stands in awe of Thy name ; and he who keeps it mentions it with fear, with purity, and with holiness. For according to Thy glory didst Thou hide it from the multitude of the sons of men, and it is transmitted only to him who is meek and of lowly spirit ; who fears God, does not get angry, and does not insist upon his ways. Yet in every generation didst Thou make plain part of the mystery thereof.

X. NATHAN HA-BABLI

[A scholar who flourished in Babylon in the tenth century. His descriptions of the Babylonian academies are obviously those of an eye-witness.]

The Installation of an Exilarch[1]

When the community agreed to appoint an exilarch, the two heads of the academies, with their pupils, the heads of the community, and the elders assembled in the house of a prominent man in Babylon, one of the great men of the generation, as, for instance, Netira, or a similar man. That man in whose house the meeting took place was honored thereby, and it was regarded as a mark of distinction; his esteem was enhanced, when the great men and the elders assembled in his house.

On Thursday they assembled in the synagogue, blessed the exilarch, and placed their hands on him. They blew the horn, that all the people, small and great, might hear. When the people heard the proclamation, every member of the community sent him a present, according to his power and means. All the heads of the community and the wealthy members sent him magnificent clothes and beautiful ornaments, vessels of silver and vessels of gold, each man according to his ability. The exilarch prepared a banquet on Thursday and on Friday, giving all kinds of food, and all kinds of drinks, and all kinds of dainties, as, for instance, different kinds of sweetmeats.

[1] Neubauer, *Mediæval Jewish Chronicles,* vol. II., pp. 83, *seq.*

When he arose on Sabbath morning to go to the synagogue, many of the prominent men of the community met him to go with him to the synagogue. At the synagogue a wooden pulpit had been prepared for him on the previous day, the length of which was seven cubits, and the breadth of which was three cubits. They spread over it magnificent coverings of silk, blue, purple, and scarlet, so that it was entirely covered, and nothing was seen of it. Under the pulpit there entered distinguished youths, with melodious and harmonious voices, who were well-versed in the prayers and all that appertains thereto. The exilarch was concealed in a certain place together with the heads of the academies, and the youths stood under the pulpit. No man sat there. The precentor of the synagogue would begin the prayer *Blessed be He who spoke,* and the youths, after every sentence of that prayer, would respond: ' Blessed be He.' When he chanted the Psalm of the Sabbath day,[2] they responded after him: ' It is good to give thanks unto the Lord.' All the people together read the ' verses of song,'[3] until they finished them. The precentor then arose, and began the prayer *The breath of all living,* and the youths responded after him: ' Shall bless Thy name '; he chanted a phrase, and they responded after him, until they reached the ' Kedushah,' which was said by the congregation with a low voice, and by the youths with a loud voice. Then the youths remained silent, and the precentor alone completed the prayer up to *He redeemed Israel.* All the people then stood up to say the Eighteen Benedictions. When

[2] That is, Psalm 91.
[3] That is, Psalms 145-150.

the precentor, repeating these Benedictions, reached
the 'Kedushah,' the youths responded after him with
a loud voice: 'The Holy God.' When he had completed the prayer, all the congregation sat down.
When all the people were seated, the exilarch came
out from the place where he was concealed. Seeing
him come out, all the people stood up, until he sat
down on the pulpit, which had been made for him.
Then the head of the academy of Sura came out after
him, and after exchanging courtesies with the exilarch, sat down on the pulpit. Then the head of the
academy of Pumbeditha came out, and he, too, made
a bow, and sat down at his left.

During all this time the people stood upon their
feet, until these three were properly seated: the exilarch sat in the middle, the head of the academy of
Sura at his right, and the head of the academy
of Pumbeditha at his left, empty places being left
between the heads of the academies and the exilarch. Upon his place, over his head, above the pulpit,
they spread a magnificent covering, fastened with cords
of fine linen and purple. Then the precentor put his
head under the exilarch's canopy in front of the pulpit,
and with blessings that had been prepared for him on
the preceding days he blessed him with a low voice, so
that they should be heard only by those who sat round
the pulpit, and by the youths who were under it. When
he blessed him, the youths responded after him with a
loud voice: 'Amen!' All the people were silent until
he had finished his blessings.

Then the exilarch would begin to expound matters
appertaining to the biblical portion of that day, or
would give permission to the head of the academy

of Sura to deliver the exposition, and the head of the academy of Sura would give permission to the head of the academy of Pumbeditha. They would thus show deference to one another, until the head of the academy of Sura began to expound. The interpreter stood near him, and repeated his words to the people. He expounded with awe, closing his eyes, and wrapping himself up with his tallith, so that his forehead was covered. While he was expounding, there was not in the congregation one that opened his mouth, or chirped, or uttered a sound. If he became aware that any one spoke, he would open his eyes, and fear and terror would fall upon the congregation. When he finished his exposition, he would begin with a question, saying: 'Verily, thou needest to learn.' And an old man who was wise, understanding, and experienced would stand up, and make a response on the subject, and sit down. Then the precentor stood up, and recited the Kaddish. When he reached the words *during your life and in your days,* he would say: 'During the life of our prince the exilarch, and during your life, and during the life of all the house of Israel.'

When he had finished the Kaddish, he would bless the exilarch, and then the heads of the academies. Having finished the blessing, he would stand up and say: 'Such and such a sum was contributed by such and such a city and its villages;' and he mentioned all the cities which sent contributions for the academy, and blessed them. Afterwards he blessed the men who busied themselves in order that the contributions should reach the academies. Then he would take out the Book of the Law, and call up a priest, and a Levite after him. While all the people were standing, the precentor of the synagogue would bring down the Book of the Law to the exilarch, who took it in his hands, stood up, and read in it. The heads of the academies stood up with him, and the head of the academy of Sura translated it to him. Then he would give back the Book of the Law to the precentor, who returned it to the ark. When the precentor reached the ark, he sat down in his place, and then all the men sat down in their places. After the exilarch the instructors read in the Book of the Law, and they were followed by the pupils of the heads of the academies; but the heads of the academies themselves did not read on that day, because someone else preceded them. When the Maftir read the last portion, a prominent and wealthy man stood near him, and translated it. This was a mark of distinction and honor for that man. When he finished reading, the precentor again blessed the exilarch by the Book of the Law, and all the readers who were experienced and well-versed in the prayers stood round the ark, and said: ' Amen! ' Afterwards he blessed the two heads of the academies, and returned the Book of the Law to its place. They then prayed the additional prayer, and left the synagogue.

XI. JOSEPH B. ISAAC IBN ABITOR

[Flourished in Spain during the tenth century. Owing to some quarrels, he left his native country, and went to Damascus. He was an eminent talmudic scholar and liturgic poet, and is said to have translated the entire Talmud into Arabic. Only a small number of his poems have been preserved, but they tend to show that he was a skilful poet with intense religious fervor. Some of them are of ingenious and complicated structure.]

1. Hymn Based on Psalm 120 [1]

O God, be gracious unto me on the day I hasten to praise Thee; forgive my sins, and judge me not according to my deeds; when with a Song of Ascents I cry to Thee, make clear to me: *'In my distress I called unto the Lord, and He answered me.'*

For Thee, O God, my soul has ever pined; through the abundance of my sins I have no respite; wipe off, I pray Thee, all my sins, the known and the unknown,—*O Lord, deliver my soul from lying lips, from a deceitful tongue.*

I said unto deceitful Uz [2]: 'Shalt thou for ever walk upright in thy wantonness? Gehenna is prepared for thee as thy apportioned lot.—*What shall be given unto thee, and what shall be done more unto thee, thou deceitful tongue?'*

[1] The following four poems are from a manuscript in the library of the Dropsie College, and are probably the first of a series of fifteen based on the fifteen Songs of Ascents (Psalms 120-134). The first stanza of each poem bears the author's name in acrostic, while the remaining stanzas are in alphabetic order, three letters being disposed of in each stanza. The fourth line is a verse, or part thereof, from the Psalm upon which the poem is based.

[2] That is, Edom. (Comp. Genesis 22. 21), hence Rome.

My presumptuous sins are marked before Thee; they
are bound up in bundles, engraved, and sealed.   Prepare a feast for them that are benign to the guileless
people;—*sharp arrows of the mighty, with coals of
broom!*

Majestic Lord, before Thee are my sorrows; among
the multitude of thorns I am well-nigh destroyed.
But a short while I lived in magnificent dwellings;
*woe is me, that I sojourn with Meshech, that I dwell
beside the tents of Kedar.*

All my oppressors smite me with horror; in the
presence of my enemies I feel deeply ashamed; all
the backsliders hate me with an everlasting hate; *my
soul hath full long had her dwelling with him that
hateth peace.*

O Most High, console Thy people that is discon-
solate; to her that is unpitied turn Thou, and be merciful.   My adversaries say: 'No comfort shalt thou
ever see.'—*I am all peace; but when I speak, they
are for war.*

Whenever it is time for praise, I cry to Thee, my
God; as I set forth my prayers, show Thy kindness
unto me.   To praise Thee, O Praised One, I kept
awake at night—accept Thou then my prayer with
the Song of Ascents.

2. Hymn Based on Psalm 121

When I come, O Creator, to proclaim Thy unity,
turn unto me!   Forgive my sins, and heed not my
wicked thoughts; with this my Song of Ascents I
cry unto Thee, O my Crown.   *I will lift up mine eyes
unto the mountains: from whence shall my help
come?*

Woe to the daughter who derides the ancients of the earth; but when I hear her mockery, I boldy answer thus: My Redeemer lives for ever; He dwells in the lofty skies—*my help cometh from the Lord, who made heaven and earth.*'

The persecutor smites the multitudes who extol Thee (behold, they have no other hope but in Thy words alone); presumptuously he mocks the words of Thy Psalms: *He will not suffer thy foot to be moved: He that keepeth thee will not slumber.*

When the wanton ones take counsel together, they plan to destroy the remnant of Ariel; but Israel says: Trust ye in God our Redeemer;—*behold, He that keepeth Israel doth neither slumber nor sleep.*

May now the trust of Thy believers be made strong and firm, according to the psalmist's words who sings Thy songs of joy: When terror seizes thee, the Lord shall be thy refuge; *the Lord is thy keeper; the Lord is thy shade upon thy right hand.*

My trust I put in Thee, O Dweller in the skies above; I stay myself upon the psalmist's words who sings jubilantly: In thy Creator put thy trust, always rely on Him; *the sun shall not smite thee by day, nor the moon by night.*

The multitude of Thy saints come before Thee; they loudly sing Thy praises in Thy holy sanctuaries; the remnant of them that seek Thee say to one another: '*The Lord shall keep thee from all evil; He shall keep thy soul.*'

All Thy beloved ones together raise their voice, and say: 'With perfect heart sing ye unto the Living God; He who understands all secrets will hear your cry; *The Lord shall guard thy going out and thy coming in, from this time forth and for ever.'*

3. Hymn Based on Psalm 122

When I draw nigh to extol Thee amidst a poor and needy people, strengthen Thou my remnant scattered in all regions. With this my Song of Ascents I cry to Thee, O King: *I rejoiced when they said unto me: ' Let us go unto the house of the Lord.'*

For my perversity I have been given twofold punishment; announce Thou consolations to the barefoot people.[3] The people, whose feet Thou makest strong, shall proclaim Thy greatness;—*our feet are standing within thy gates, O Jerusalem!*

Establish Thou the pillars of Thy desolate temple; the measurements thereof make wondrous fair, and wide, and long. This miracle shall strike with confusion him who destroyed the desirable things thereof: *Jerusalem that was built as a city that is compact together.*

The righteous song regard with favor; may it be Thy will to gladden with the redeemer's coming them that trust in Thee. Thy banished children shall go up to erect Ariel, *whither the tribes went up, even the tribes of the Lord, as a testimony unto Israel.*

Destroy them that strive with me, and increase their tribulations; enslave the tyrant;—*for there were set thrones for judgment, the thrones of the house of David.*

Bring good tidings to them that sanctify Thee and sing Thy words—they that are led by a fiery wall near Thee; I shall rejoice near Thy shield, and hear Thy

[3] That is, Israel mourning for the temple.

pleasing words: '*Pray for the peace of Jerusalem; may they prosper that love thee.*'

O city of the Lord, rejoice, and increase thy lays; burst forth with song, exult, make thy melodies great; I shall fill thy utterances with joy and exultation; *peace be within thy walls, and prosperity within thy palaces.*

They that wait for Thy utterance shall lift up their voice together; they that sanctify Thy unity shall sing new melodies; they that are satisfied with bliss from Thee shall proclaim peace; *for my brethren and companions' sakes I will now say: 'Peace be within thee.'*

Increase the glory of the stronghold in Thy border; mayest Thou hear from Thy habitation the praises which we utter; may the wisdom of Thy anointed be spoken in Thy temple: *for the sake of the house of the Lord our God I will seek thy good.*

4. Hymn Based on Psalm 123

When I seek Thee amongst them that proclaim Thy unity twice, that hope for the day of Thy wonders to be redeemed from their two exiles, I pour out my heart like water in the Song of Ascents; *unto Thee I lift mine eyes, O Thou that art enthroned in the heavens.*

O Give ear unto Thy people's groans and hear their supplications, when they draw near to Thee to set forth their hymns of praise, and when, humbly kneeling, they lift their eyes to Thee: *behold, as the eyes of servants unto the hand of their master.*

Deliver from destruction them that seek Thy face; hasten Thy salvation in due time to them that pray for it; look on the afflicted people's woes, when it renders thanks to Thee: *as the eyes of a maiden unto the hand of her mistress.*

Remember Thy lovingkindness, O God, our Shield; O pity us, have mercy, and forgive our sins; O Thou that art pure, we ever seek Thee, answer us;—*so our eyes look unto the Lord our God, until He be gracious unto us.*

Despise not the woes of the remnant of the plundered ones, for the tents of Uz and Buz devoured and destroyed them; Jeush hastes to trample on us, and Buz[4] speeds to spoil; *be gracious unto us, O Lord, be gracious unto us; for we are full sated with contempt.*

Tribulations have beset us, and have humbled our heads; we have been left groaning, entangled in our snares. Through the abundance of our guilt, with filth and bitterness *our soul is full sated.*

The company of the needy ones, that have escaped and still remain, hope for Thy righteous acts, O Highest of all high. They that are filled with tribulations set forth their meditations;—*with the scorning of those that are at ease and with the contempt of the proud oppressors.*

[4] All these are tribes of Gentiles. Comp. Genesis 22. 21; 36. 18.

XII. HAI B. SHERIRA GAON

[The last Gaon of the academy at Pumbeditha. He was an eminent authority on the Talmud, and numerous responsa written by him are still extant. He was the author of commentaries on talmudic treatises and of a dictionary of difficult words occurring in the Bible, Targum, and Talmud. He also acquired fame as a poet, and was one of the first to employ the Arabic metre in Hebrew poetry. He died 1038.]

Maxims and Admonitions [1]

Let thy tongue be imprisoned in thy mouth, and in company be thou like one that is mute.

Loose not a lion that is bound by thy chain, for if thou settest him free, he will devour thee.

Cast not thy gaze upon thy neighbor's wife, and thine own helpmate keep inside the house; it is glory for women and grace for men that women should not look upon strange men.

Make no partnership, though thou needest aid; transact no business with thy kith and kin.

Dwell not too long by the river; turn to the mountain on account of the rain.

Sow goodness, that thou mayest reap pleasantness, and thy reward from God shall be complete.

Be perfect and upright with God, and seek not that which is too high.

Keep away from imbeciles, from deaf and dumb, and from women; have no quarrels with them.

If thou hast not acquired wisdom and understanding, sit near the judges of the people when they preside.

[1] Philipp's edition, lines 109-136. For reasons, which do not appear to be cogent, Hai's authorship of these maxims has been doubted.

Be not ashamed to learn and to seek knowledge; be a tail to the wise, so that thou mayest become a head.

It is wisdom to tread in the ways of faith; to fear God and to depart from evil is understanding.

Be near the judges of the community, and buy thy things in the proper manner of transaction. For thy possessions choose good witnesses,—they will relieve thee from strife.

It is better for thee to visit mourners than to go to the house of feasting and rejoicing.

Reveal not to an enemy that which is in thy heart; uproot his enmity, if thou hatest him not.

Inquire about the sick, and visit them with a cure; speak comfortingly unto embittered men.

Depart from quarrel, and flee from strife, and stand not upon the verge of a pit and an abyss.

Honor thy parents, and also thy kinsmen and all that seek their peace.

If thou drawest nigh unto the shadow of a king, know that thou standest near a lion. Then other men shall be exceedingly afraid of thee, but thy fear shall also be great and awful.

Thou shouldst not hold the horns of a fierce bull, and do not seize the bridle of a lion.

Grieve not if unto thee a daughter is born; trust in God, exult and rejoice in thy lot. At times a daughter is better than a son; she is good and pure to her parents. Take delight in whatsoever comes from God, and say: 'This also is for the best!'

It is better that thy daughter should go down to the grave as a maiden than that she should beseech a man.

Buy thee a dwelling among the upright; depart from the habitation of the covetous and envious.

XIII. SAMUEL HA-NAGID

[Born at Cordova 993, and died at Granada 1055. He was famous as a poet, Halakist, and philologist, and was the author of a treatise on the methodology of the Talmud. Some medieval Jewish critics considered him the greatest Hebrew poet. This view, however, cannot be maintained, as he was certainly surpassed by Ibn Gebirol and Judah ha-Levi. He was for some time vizier at the court of King Habus. His poems, perhaps more than those of any other poet of that epoch, resemble the Arabic poems very closely.]

1. On Leaving Cordova[1]

The soul is deprived of that which it desires, and that which it asks is withheld from it. Although the body is plump, and fed, and fat, the glorious soul is not yet satisfied. A humble man walks on the earth, and yet his thoughts reach unto the skies. Of what avail is it to man to have his body's pleasures, while his soul is distressed? Some friends there are who harm and profit not; they have big bodies, but their minds are small. They think that to increase my riches I depart from my dwelling-place and roam about—though the locks of my head are dishevelled and mine eye is painted with night's stibium. My friends know not the secrets of my heart; indeed my friends spoke not knowingly. Their soul knows nought, nor does it understand; it is like the soul of a cloven-footed beast.

Shall he refrain himself, whose soul is like a moon, and, like the moon, strives to soar high? And shall

[1] Harkavy's edition No. 15; Brody's edition No. 36. It is an excellent specimen of the Fakhr (self-glorification) poems of the Arabs.

he rest until he girds his loins with her wings, as one girds on a cloth, and till his deeds are heard throughout the world, and like the ocean is his fame increased?

I swear by God and by His worshippers (assuredly, my like shall keep his oath) that I will ascend the rocks on foot, and go down to the deepest pit; The borders of the desert will I join, and cross the ocean in a boat with sails; I shall roam about until I soar and rise to a height that forever shall be known. With terrors shall I then inspire my foes, but my friends shall find salvation in me. The ears of freemen shall I bore through [2] as slaves', and mine ear, too, shall be bored through by my friends.

I have a soul that sustains my friends, but from my adversaries it is withheld. In it there is for thee a garden filled with friendship, planted by the brook of love; it is that friendship which is kept from early youth, like a signet fixed in a ring; it is engraved like the green gravings in a window cut out in the door of a palace.

May God be with thee as thou lovest, and may thy soul, which He loves, be redeemed from the hand of foes. May the God of deliverance send thee salvation, till there be no sun and moon!

2. On Having Been Saved in Mid-Ocean from a Tunny Fish [3]

Shall he that falls and stumbles rise again, and he that roams and wanders find repose? Shall I be

[2] Comp. Exodus 21. 6.
[3] Harkavy's edition, No. 23; Brody's edition, No. 39. Some lines are missing in the place indicated by the asterisks. Then follows a graphic description of the tunny fish.

raised yet once more, although my feet stumbled, and my ankle slipped?

In my soul are all the things that offer help and consolation to the stricken souls; but confusion reigns in the souls of them that came to gloat over me in the day of my discomfiture. They think that troublous times never change, a waste land shall not be inhabited. Yet God does raise them that He humbled and brought low; and He has mysteries, His way is hid.

O hear this word, and know that not in vain does God keep me alive upon the earth; and then shalt thou receive the evil days with cheerful heart, closed mouth, and bridled thought. Let thine ear be deaf to dissenters, and thine eye closed from seeing backsliders, who are like Hofni in Shiloh,[4] or like Zimri with the Midianite woman,[5] or Onan[6] with his brother's wife.

O hear this word, exalt God in thy house, and on thy way, whilst thou sittest or standest.

*   *   *

Her head is as a row boat in size, with a countenance raised very high; she has eyes like fountains, a nostril like a furnace, and temples like a wall. Her mouth is deep and wide like a cave; when thirsty, she pours a stream into it. Her lips resemble two inflated skin-bottles, and between them is a hole like that of a torn garment. White is her body, green her back; her neck is like a tower, her belly is like a heap. Her fins are like a keen-edged sword; her scales look like a red buckler. To them that watch, her structure is like a rock projecting in mid-ocean.

[4] Comp. 1 Samuel 2. 22, 34.
[5] Numbers 25. 6, 14.
[6] Genesis 38. 9, 10.

When she came swimming round about the boat, no
one uttered aught, nor breathed a word. Then she
drew nigh unto the sides of the boat, and stood on her
tail which was as a cedar or a vine.

The hearts of all men melted like wax, like water,
or a stream that is swept away. Through grief I stilled
me like a lamb that becomes mute on the day of
slaughter. Then I thought of my God, while others
at my side thought of gods like Ashima.⁷ I said: ' It
is true, in such or such a way transgressions ensnare
the guilty soul; though Jonah through piety was
vomited from the sea on land, but what am I? My God,
stay Thy wrath, for this calamity awakened me (for I
had been slumbering). But if I deserve this punishment, may it be an atonement for my great guilt.'

She then sank into the water, like the host which
God had cast and thrown into the sea, and came beneath to overthrow the boat; (all hearts stood still,
and every breath was gone). But God rebuked her,
so that she returned in a moment to her abode in the
depth of the sea. Thus to small worms He brought
salvation, upon a beam daubed all around with pitch.
The dead restored He from the grave, and with His
high and lofty hand He saved the drowning.

All men who know the ocean marvelled, and said:
' Wherefore, and how did these escape? for hitherto
no boat has yet been saved from this accursed mon-
ster of the deep.'

I answered them: ' Thus God's redemption is majestic and complete to them that know the glory of His
splendor ; He works salvation for them that know Him,
and takes vengeance upon them that provoke Him.

⁷ Comp. 2 Kings 17. 30.

His are the sea, the beasts, and the waters of the great
deep—all of them He hung on nought. What is this
beast against the Lord, who made her reign supreme,
and gave her strength and might?'

To God I will render the thanks of them that are
redeemed—it shall be set and put in my mouth. I
declare that, unlike created things, my Rock has no beginning and no end; I declare that the dead shall be
quickened, when the end of the mysterious heptad [8]
comes; that Moses and the Torah which is in our hands
are true—it is marked with perfection; that the words
of our sages are straight and upright, their Talmud and
their Mishnah are pleasant; that there is a goodly reward for the pure in the next world, a recompense for
them that die for the sake of the traditional law. God
has dominion over land and sea, over heaven, the
Great Bear, and Pleiades. His fear is put upon my
countenance, and His Torah is perfect in my heart.

[8] Comp. Daniel 9. 24-27.

6

XIV. SOLOMON B. JUDAH IBN GEBIROL

[Deep thinker and lyric poet. One of the most original and noblest minds of medieval Jewry. He was born at Malaga about 1021, and died at Valencia about 1058. In his philosophic works and in his poems which are still extant one discerns a spirit that strives to soar high and to attain to the loftiest state of mental development. In his soul mystic and rational elements are wonderfully blended. He had great influence upon subsequent writers.]

1. On Leaving Saragossa[1]

My throat became dried from crying, my tongue cleaved unto my palate; my heart flutters because of my great anguish and pain. Great is my sorrow, that it no longer allows mine eyes to slumber.

To whom shall I speak and complain? to whom shall I declare my grief? Would there were one to comfort and to pity me, who would hold my right hand! I would pour out my heart to him, and would relate some of my woes. Perchance by uttering my grief the tempest of my heart may subside a little.

O thou who inquirest about my peace, draw nigh, and hearken! My roaming is as the sea's. If thy heart were as adamant, it would melt from my affliction. How canst thou think I am alive, while thou knowest my languishment? Alas! I dwell in the midst of a people that thinks my right hand is my left. I am interred, but not in a desert—my coffin is within my house. I am motherless and fatherless, distressed and lonely,

---

[1] Dukes' edition, No. 1. The poet complains of his uncongenial surroundings. He is misunderstood by his neighbors, because he strives to attain to knowledge.

young and poor. Alone, without a brother, I have no
other friend but my thoughts. I mix my flowing tears
with blood, and then my wine is mixed with tears. I
thirst for a friend, but I shall be consumed ere my thirst
is slaked. The heavens and their host prevent me from
attaining my desire. I am counted like a stranger or
sojourner, my dwelling is amongst ostriches ; among the
crooked and the fools, who think that they are very
wise : the one gives to drink the venom of asps, the
other, flattering, smooths the head ; but he lays an am-
bush in his heart, though he says to thee : ' I pray thee,
my lord.' They are a people whose fathers I would disdain to set with the dogs of my flock. Their faces never
blush with shame, unless they are dyed with scarlet.
Like giants are they in their sight, in my sight they are
like locusts. When I take up my parable, they chide me,
as they would chide a Greek : ' Speak a tongue that
we understand, for this speech is of an Ashkelonite.'

I shall now crush them as mire, for my tongue is
like a sharp spear. If their ear is deaf to me, of what
avail can be my bell ? Unworthy are their necks to be
adorned with the gold of my crescents.

Oh that the fools would open their mouth to receive
the spring-rain of my clouds ! My perfume would I
drop on them, my saffron and my cinnamon. Woe
unto knowledge, woe to me ! In the midst of such a
people do I dwell ! They count the knowledge of
God as witchcraft and as sorcery.

I therefore lament and wail, I lie all night in sackcloth. I am bowed down as a bulrush, and fast on the
second and fifth days of every week. What shall I
hope for, while I live ? in what then shall I put my
faith ? Mine eye roams about in this world, but it
beholds not what I desire. Oh death is precious in

my sight, because I disdain this earth. If my heart turns to her ways, may my tongue cleave to my palate! My soul rejects her glory, for her honor is disgrace in mine eyes. I never shall rejoice in her, my pride shall not exult in her, even if the constellations would call to me: 'Turn in, and sit with us, O lord.' For this earth has become to me as a yoke upon my neck. What else is left me in this world, except to endure my blindness?

My soul complains aloud, for it found not as yet my abode. I am weary of my life, and loathe that my flesh should lord over me. For its rejoicing is my grief; and when it sorrows, I rejoice. I seek to know, and I shall find true knowledge when my flesh and vigor are gone. For after grief comes relief, after leanness comes my nourishment.

All my life I shall search and seek the commands of Solomon my ancestor. Perchance He who lays bare deep things will reveal wisdom to mine eye; for this alone is my portion from all my labor and wealth.

2. A Vow to Seek Wisdom [2]

A soul whose raging tempests wildly rise, whither shall she send her meditations? She rages, and is like a flame of fire, whose smoke constantly ascends. This time her meditations are like a wheel that turns around on the earth and the multitudes thereof, or like the seas wherein the earth's foundations were fastened: 'How canst thou be so strong and filled with courage, that thou disdainest a place upon the stars? From

[2] Dukes' edition, No. 7. The poet declares that, in spite of all obstacles and discouragement, he will seek wisdom and strive to make himself as perfect as possible.

the path of wisdom turn thou away thy heart; the world shall then smooth thy path for thee.'

Oh comfort ye my soul for that, my friends, and likewise for her sorrows comfort her; she thirsts for a man of prudence, but finds not a man to slake her thirst. Seek ye amongst the men of fame, perchance there may be one to grant her desires. If this world sins against me, my heart will regard it disdainfully. If it cannot see my light with its eye, let the world then be contented with its blindness. But afterwards, if it appeases me, I shall turn round, and forgive its sins. The earthly sphere would then be good; the hand of Time would place no yoke upon the wise.

Oh too much wrong didst thou commit; long have the gourds been as cedars of the earth. Despise the vile ones of the people, for stones are less burdensome to me than they. Cut off the tail of them that say to me: 'Where is then wisdom and her votaries?' Oh that the world would judge them aright! oh that it would give food unto her sons! They would then rest, not toil, and would attain their goal, without knowing worldly joys. Some took the sun's daughters, and begot folly, but they were not its sons-in-law.[3]

Why do ye chide me for my understanding, O ye thorns and briers of the earth? If wisdom is of light esteem to you, vile and despised are ye in her sight. Though she is closed, and reaches not your heart, lo, I shall open her chests. How shall I now abandon wisdom, since God's spirit made a covenant between us? or how shall she forsake me, since she is like a mother to me and I am the child of her old age? or like an ornament which adorns the soul, or like a

[3] This seems to be an allusion to those who adopted false doctrines.

necklace on her neck. How can ye say to me: 'Take
off thy ornaments, and remove the precious chain from
her neck'? In her my heart rejoices, and is glad, because her rivers of delights are pure. Throughout my
life I shall make my soul ascend until her abode is beyond the clouds. For she adjured me not to rest, until I
find the knowledge of her Master.

3. The Royal Crown [4]

This my prayer may avail a man to learn righteousness and purity; therein I declared wonders of the
living God, briefly, not at length. I placed this hymn
above all my hymns; wherefore I named it 'Royal
Crown.'

Wonderful are Thy works, and that my soul knows
right well! Thine, O Lord, is the greatness, and the
power, and the glory, and the eminence, and the
majesty. Thine, O Lord, is the kingdom, and Thou
art the One exalted as head above all; and Thine are
riches and glory. Unto Thee do the creatures from
above and beneath testify that they shall perish, but
Thou shalt endure. Thine is that power whose mystery
our minds fail to fathom, for Thou art too mighty for
us. Thine is the hiding-place of might, the mystery
and the foundation. Thine is the name which is concealed from the men of wisdom, and the power which
sustains the universe on nothing, and the ability to
bring every hidden thing to light. Thine is the lovingkindness which is great toward Thy creatures, and
the bliss which is stored up for them that fear Thee.

---

[4] This is the first part of that beautiful composition in
rhymed prose. It has been incorporated in the Sephardic
ritual for the eve of the Day of Atonement. The biblical
verses are introduced with wonderfully artistic skill.

Thine are the mysteries which no intellect nor mind can contain, and the life over which decay has no dominion, and the throne which is exalted above all the highest, and the habitation which is concealed in the height of the hiding-place. Thine is the existence from the shadow of whose light every being was created, of which we say: ' Under its shadow we live.' Thine are the two worlds between which Thou didst set a boundary: the first for deeds and the second for recompense. Thine is the recompense which Thou didst store up and hide for the righteous, for when Thou didst see that it was good, Thou didst conceal it.

Thou art one, the first of every number, and the foundation of every structure. Thou art one, and at the mystery of Thy oneness the wise are perplexed, for they know not what it is. Thou art one, and Thy oneness can neither increase nor decrease; it can neither be diminished, nor can aught be added to it. Thou art one, but not such a one as can be possessed or numbered; for neither increase nor change, neither qualification nor attribute can be conceived of Thee. Thou art one, but my imagination fails to set a limit and a bound about Thee; I have therefore said: ' I will take heed to my ways, that I sin not with my tongue.' Thou art one, too high and too exalted to be brought low and to fall, for how can the One fall?

Thou art existent, but the hearing of the ear and the sight of the eye cannot perceive Thee; nor can the How? the Wherefore? or the Whence? be applied to Thee. Thou art existent, but by Thyself, and there is none other with Thee. Thou art existent, and hadst been before time was, and didst abide without space. Thou art existent, but Thy mystery is hidden, who can reach it? exceeding deep, who can find it out?

Thou art living, but not from any fixed time, nor from any known period. Thou art living, but not through a soul and breath, for Thou art the soul of the soul. Thou art living, but not as the life of man who is like to vanity, and whose end is moth and vermin. Thou art living, and he who reaches Thy mystery shall find everlasting delight: he shall eat, and live for ever.

Thou art great, and compared with Thy greatness all greatness is humbled, and every excellence is faulty. Thou art too great for any thought, and too sublime for any composition. Thou art greater than all greatness, and exalted above all blessing and praise.

Thou art mighty, and among Thy creatures and beings there is none that can do according to Thy works and according to Thy mighty acts. Thou art mighty, and Thine is the absolute power which changes not and alters not. Thou art mighty, and because of the abundance of Thy might Thou dost pardon even in the time of Thy indignant wrath, and dost defer Thine anger to sinners. Thou art mighty, yet Thy tender mercies are over all Thy creatures: these are Thy mighty deeds that were of old.

Thou art light, and the eyes of every pure soul shall behold Thee; but the clouds of iniquity shall hide Thee from its eyes. Thou art the light which is hidden in this world, but shall be revealed in the high and beautiful world; on the mount of the Lord shall it be seen.

Thou art most high, and the eye of the intellect yearns and longs for Thee; but it can only see the utmost thereof, and cannot see the whole.

Thou art the God of gods, and all Thy creatures are Thy witnesses, and for the glory of this name every creature is obliged to worship Thee. Thou art God, and all the beings are Thy servants and Thy worshippers; yet Thy glory is not diminished because of them that worship aught beside Thee; for the intention of them all is to attain unto Thee, but they are as the blind: they set their faces toward the way of the King; but they wander out of the way: one sinks into the pit of destruction, and another falls into the abyss; they all think that they have reached their goal, but they labored in vain. But Thy servants are as the clear-sighted who walk in the straight path: they turn not from the way to the right hand or to the left until they come to the court of the King's house. Thou art God, supporting the beings with Thy divinity, and sustaining the creatures with Thy unity. Thou art God, and there is no distinction between Thy divinity, and Thy unity, and Thy eternity, and Thy existence; for it is all one mystery: although the names of each one are different, they all go unto one place.

Thou art wise, and wisdom, which is the fountain of life, emanates from Thee; compared with Thy wisdom, every man is brutish and without knowledge. Thou art wise, prior to all first beings, and even wisdom was Thy nursling. Thou art wise, but Thou didst not learn from another, nor didst Thou acquire wisdom from any one beside Thee. Thou art wise, and from Thy wisdom didst Thou set apart the pre-destined will, as a workman and an artist, to draw forth the emanation of existence from non-existence (as the light, issuing from the eye, emanates and draws from the fountain of light without a bucket), and it made all things without instruments. It hewed and engraved, cleansed and purified; it called unto non-existence, and it was cleft in twain: unto existence, and it was established; unto the universe, and it was stretched out. It meted out heaven with the span; its hand joined the pavilion of the spheres, and fastened the curtains over the creatures with the loops of potentiality. Its power reaches as far as the edge of the curtain, the outermost creation, which is the extreme end of the coupling.

XV. BAHYA B. JOSEPH IBN PAKUDA

[Philosopher, talmudic scholar, and liturgic poet. Difference of opinion exists as to the time when he flourished. It is usually accepted that he lived in the eleventh century. But arguments, though by no means conclusive, have been brought forth to prove that he lived a century later. To him is due the credit of having been the author of the first Jewish system of ethics. His ethical work *Hobot ha-Lebabot* (Duties of the Heart), which was written in Arabic, has always been a great favorite in its Hebrew translation.]

Pious Reflections and Admonitions to the Soul [1]

Bless the Lord, O my soul; and all that is within me, bless His holy name.

O my soul, march on with strength, and bless thy Creator. Prepare a supplication for Him, and pour out thy meditation before Him. Awake from thy sleep, and consider thy place, whence thou camest, and whither thou goest.

O my soul, awake from thy slumber, and utter a song to thy Creator; sing praises unto His name, declare his wonders, and fear Him wherever thou dwellest.

O my soul, be not as the horse, or as the mule, which have no understanding; nor shouldst thou be as a drunkard that is fast asleep, or as a man that is stupefied; for out of the fountain of understanding wast thou formed, and from the spring of wisdom wast thou taken; from a holy place wast thou brought forth, and from the city of the mighty, from heaven, wast thou taken out by God.

[1] This beautiful prose poem has been frequently printed in some Hebrew prayer-books.

O my soul, put on garments of prudence, and gird
on a girdle of understanding, and free thyself from
the vanities of thy body, in which thou dwellest. Let
not thy heart beguile thee with the sweetness of its
desires, and let it not allure thee with the visions of
its pleasures which melt away like water that runs
apace. Remember that the beginning of these pleasures is without help or profit, and their end is shame
and also reproach.

O my soul, run to and fro through the streets of
thy understanding, and go about in the chambers of
thy wisdom, and come unto the structure of the building of thy imagery, whose foundation is in dust; is it
not a despised body and a carcass trodden under foot?
It is formed out of a troubled fountain and a corrupted spring, built of a fetid drop; it is burned
with fire, it is cut down. It is an unformed substance
resembling a worm, it is nought but terror. It is
kept in a foul womb, closed up in an impure belly; it
is born with pangs and sorrows to see trouble and
vanities. All day long it covets pleasures, and departs
from instruction and from commandments; it comes
in the dark, and goes away in the dark; it is a poor,
needy, and destitute wayfarer. It has no knowledge
without thee, and no understanding beside thee.
While alive, it is dust; and when it dies, it is ashes.
As long as it lives, worms surround it, and when its
end comes, vermin and clods of dust cover it. It
cannot discern between its right hand and its left
hand; its lot is hidden in the ground. Go thou, therefore, and reign over it, for sovereignty is meet unto
the children of wisdom, and the foolish is a servant
to the wise of heart. Walk not in the stubbornness
of thy wicked heart, be not ensnared by its counsels,

and despise the gain of its frauds; trust not in oppression, and become not vain in robbery; for oppression makes a wise man foolish, and a bribe destroys the heart.

O my soul, set thy heart toward the highway, even the way by which thou didst go; for all was made of dust, and indeed unto dust shall all return. Every thing that was created and fashioned has an end and a goal to return unto the ground, whence it was taken. Life and death are brothers that dwell together; they are joined to one another; they cling together, so that they cannot be sundered. They are joined together by the two extremes of a frail bridge over which all created beings travel: life is the entrance, and death is the exit thereof. Life builds, and death demolishes; life sows, and death reaps; life plants, and death uproots; life joins together, and death separates; life links together, and death scatters. Know, I pray thee, and see that also unto thee shall the cup pass over, and thou shalt soon go out from the lodging-place which is on the way, when time and chance befall thee, and thou returnest to thine everlasting home. On that day shalt thou delight in thy work, and take thy reward in return for thy labor wherein thou hast toiled in this world, whether it be good or bad. Therefore hearken, I pray thee, and consider, and incline thine ear; forget thy people and thy father's house. Arise, and sing unto thy King all thy day and all thy night; lift up thy hands toward Him, and bow down unto Him with thy face to the ground; let thine eyelids gush out with waters, and kneel thou upon thy knees; the King may perchance desire thy beauty, and lift up His countenance unto thee, and give thee peace. He will be gracious unto thee in the days of thy affliction in this world, and also after thou hast returned to thy rest. For as long as thou didst live He dealt bountifully with thee.

O my soul, prepare provision in abundance, prepare not little, while thou art yet alive, and while thy hand has yet strength, because the journey is too great for thee. And say not: 'I shall prepare provision to-morrow'; for the day has declined, and thou knowest not what the next day may bring forth. Know likewise that yesterday shall never come back, and that whatever thou hast done therein is weighed, numbered, and counted. Nor shouldst thou say: 'I shall do it to-morrow'; for the day of death is hidden from all the living. Hasten to do thy task every day, for death may at any time send forth its arrow and lightning. Delay not to do thy daily task, for as a bird wanders from its nest, so does a man wander from his place. Think not with thyself that after thou hast gone forth from the prison of thy body thou wilt turn to correction from thy perpetual backsliding; for it will not be possible for thee then to do good or evil; it will not avail thee then to turn away from backsliding or to repent of wickedness, guilt, and transgression. For that world has been established to render accounts—the book of the hidden and concealed deeds which every man commits is sealed—and it has been prepared to grant a good reward to them that fear the Lord and think upon His name, and to execute the vengeance of the covenant upon them that forget God, who say unto God: 'Depart from us, for we desire not the knowledge of Thy ways. What is the Almighty, that we should serve Him? and what profit should we have, if we pray unto Him?'[2]

[2] Comp. Job 21. 14, 15.

O my soul, if thou art wise, thou art wise for thyself; and if thou scoffest, thy error remains with
thee. Hear instruction, and be wise, and refuse it
not. Lay continually to thy heart the words of
Koheleth the son of David: ' The end of the matter,
all having been heard: fear God, and keep His commandments; for this is the whole man. For God
will bring every work into judgment concerning every
hidden thing, whether it be good or whether it be
evil.' [3] Forget not that He seals up the hand of every
man, that all men whom He has made may know it.[4]
Remember likewise that there is no darkness and no
thick darkness wherein the workers of iniquity may
hide themselves.[5] Seek the Lord thy Maker with all
thy might and strength. Seek righteousness, seek
meekness; it may be that thou wilt be hidden in the
day of God's anger, and in the day of His fierce
wrath, and that thou wilt shine as the brightness of
the firmament and as the sun when it goes forth in
its might. The sun of righteousness with healing
in its wings shall shine upon thee. Now arise, go and
make supplication unto thy Lord, and take up a
melody unto thy God. Praise thou God, for it is
good to sing praises to our God; for it is pleasant, and
praise is comely.

[3] Ecclesiastes 12. 13, 14.
[4] Comp. Job 37. 7.
[5] Comp. Job 34. 22.

XVI. AHIMAAZ B. PALTIEL

[Liturgic poet and author of a family chronicle. He was born at Capua, Italy, 1017, and died at Oria about 1060. His Chronicles (*Sefer Yuhasin*) is an important source for the history of the early Jewish settlement in Italy.]

Shephatiah Before His Death on Rosh ha-Shanah Declares that the Tyrant Basil Is Dead [1]

And Rabbi Shephatiah was old and well stricken with age; and God blessed him with all pleasant qualities. The Dweller of the high heavens gave him the Torah as a possession, and made him great with riches and immense wealth. He endowed him with a son who was worthy and perfect; the father and the son were faultless. With them was Rabbi Hananel who was great and perfect; they were all steadfast in the fear of God. They were brothers and friends, and were pleasant in their friendship. They continually occupied themselves with the Torah and with the commandments and lovingly fulfilled God's statutes. They exalted their King with strength and with glory, and magnified their Maker with honor and majesty, and made for their Creator a wreath, and a crown, and a diadem of fine gold. They ascribed strength and power to their Maker, and came in the evening and in the morning to the assembly of prayers. All the days that they were upon earth they bewailed with grief the exile and the destruction, and lamented with bitterness and desolation over the persecution.

[1] Neubauer, *Mediæval Jewish Chronicles,* vol. II., p. 123, *seq.*

They cried and made supplications to Him who turns wise men backward,[2] by whose knowledge the depths were broken up, and who established and founded the rivers and seas, that He should make foolish the knowledge of the enemy, and that He should lay his kingdom waste. They asked understanding from Him who is full of mercy, that the decree of persecution should be brought to nought and be abolished. Because of their cry which they cried to the Highest of all high, the decree did not pass across from the other side of the seas, and His servants who were perfect in His laws He delivered from filth, and dirt, and foul waters: from being made to kneel to the deaf and mute, and from worshipping the blind and sightless, and from bowing down to idols and images. He thundered with the voice of thunders upon their enemies, and was filled with indignation against their persecutors; He delivered His beloved ones from the hand of them that rise up against them; and spared their soul from the coals of broom; that they may occupy themselves with the Torah, and meditate therein, and that they may smell the savor of the spices and perfumes which are hidden and sealed up in the treasuries and storehouses, which are closed up in the Eden of the venerable and ancient fathers. Then Rabbi Shephatiah, the teacher among the wise, yielded up his soul completely to the Judge of the widows and the Father of orphans. He tasted the cup of his ancestors, which the father of the serpents caused all mortals to drink.[3]

On New Year's day, Rabbi Shephatiah, being the worthiest man in a worthy congregation, had to blow

[2] Comp. Isaiah 44. 25.
[3] Comp. Genesis 3.

the horn, for the sake of the glory of God and His
people.   That day he was feeble, bent down by illness; but all the congregation whispered to him per-
suasively: 'Our master that art clothed with light,
radiance of our splendor, light of our eyes, blow
thou the horn for us; all the days that our God will
keep thee among us no other man shall blow the
horn in our midst.'   And they burdened him with
the blowing of the horn.   He stood up, and blew the
horn; but he was without strength and power, and
the blowing of the horn did not come out in a fitting
manner.   Whereupon the righteous man cried out
aloud unto them, and justified God's judgment against
himself: 'My children, may this be a good omen
unto you; for on account of my transgressions fortune has changed against me.'   He left the synagogue
of his congregation, went to his house, and lay down
upon his bed.   And all the congregation came after
him to his bed-chamber.   He then turned his face
toward them, and thus said he unto them: ' I am going
to my eternal rest, to my lot with the ancient fathers ;
and I make known unto you, my dear sons, my three
beloved sons, that Basil[4] the oppressor and apostate is
dead.   He passes before me now, bound with chains
of fire, and is handed over to the destroying angels.
And He whose name is the Lord of hosts sent for me
to go to meet Basil, and to contend against him in
judgment, because of all the evil which he had done
unto His people, in order to cut off his name and the
name of his seed, his root, his offspring, and his
plant.'   (And they wrote down the day and the hour.
Some days later a report came that Basil who had
done evil died; in accordance with the words of the

[4] Basil I, known as the Macedonian (died 886).

righteous man did the letter arrive. For thus the emperors of Constantinople were wont to do according to their custom; when a king died, they would send an explicit letter to Bari,[5] and write down the day and the time, which brought the terrible tidings of the king's death.) 'Blessed be He who alone does wondrous things, who destroyed him from this world, and cut him off from the world to come. Blessed be His name, and blessed be the name of His glory. Now I am to be gathered unto my people, and I shall go to my place. And ye, my children, the children of my trials, all the congregation of my multitudes, may God be with you. He kills, and makes alive; He is named I AM THAT I AM, when He brings to life the righteous of Benjamin and the lion's whelp.' [6]

[5] Town in Italy.
[6] That is, Judah; comp. Genesis 49. 9.

XVII. MOSES B. JACOB IBN EZRA

[Poet, philosopher, and philologist. He wrote gracefully in Arabic and Hebrew. He was born about 1070 at Granada, and died in the first half of the twelfth century. His best works are still in manuscript, but even his published books show him to have been a man of great talent. His poetry was chiefly praised for the beauty and polish of its diction. Judah ha-Levi addressed several panegyrics to him.]

1. Dirge on the Death of His Brother [1]

Oh mourn, my soul, and with a mourning cloak be clad, and put ropes upon thy sackcloth; be gathered to go to the right and left, awake to wail and to strip off thy train. Sell thy joy forever; it shall never be redeemed, nor shall it have a jubilee. Write a bill of divorce to rejoicing, take wailing instruments instead of harps. No longer shalt thou dread the wrath of time, nor fear the burning anger of the world; for what more can it do to thee? It has harmed thee grievously, and brought thee dire distress! Now that my brother is fallen, time is powerless to do me good, or to wound me. It smote, and did not spare; it broke all thy strength and glory, as a vessel made of clay. It hurled down thy height with wrath; how canst thou say that thy lot is cast in pleasantness?

Since my brother is gone my world is no more wide; it is a prison, and the earth is like shackles. He that upheld the glory of all things, how is it that his back is now burdened with dust? Because he is gone the sun is the companion of jackals, the moon is the brother of mourning since his death.

[1] Brody, in *Steinschneider's Festschrift* (1896), p. 43 (Hebrew part).

Now shall all understand that heaven's host will fade and shrivel as a withering bud (all this shall vanish as a clod of earth, and yet the memory of his glory never shall grow old). When my brother went to the grave, I knew that all creation is but vanity.

2. Poem Addressed to One of His Noblest Friends[2]

A prisoner,[3] whose heart is made to boil like a pot by a burning flame, and whose eyes are laden with a cloud of tears! He thought to relieve his illness with his tears, but when he shed them, lo, it was rain making things to grow: a smoking furnace which, without a hand, sprinkles soot upon the brightness of his face and forehead. From his scalding tears the mountains crumble, just as when he roars the raging seas are calmed. In Edom's field he wanders without pasture (regarded by none), like lost sheep which a lion thrust aside.

For him the daughters of the Great Bear moan, for him Orion makes baldness like an eagle. The hand of time went forth against him for evil, until with wrath it banished him out of the West.

How long shall he traverse the surface of the earth? how long shall he not loose his girdle and his belt? His brothers stood at a distance to gloat over him in his distress, and all his friends broke their covenant. With willful hand they shed his blood, and how could they have thought to cover it on a rock? But when God saw his strength was spent, He appointed thy right hand, O my lord, to shelter and to cover him. In his misty night thou didst shine as a star, and he beheld the light of companionship in the gloom of exile.

[2] *Ibid.*, p. 44.
[3] The poet describes his own plight.

His feet had slipped, but when he saw thy dwelling-place, they stood up firmly as in strongholds and on rocks. He came to the midst of the garden, and through thy sweet words his soul was made secure on fields of ease. Thou art honey to the palate, sunlight to the eye of him that looks, and myrrh unto the nostril of him that smells. Thou art the foundation of kindness, glory's pillar, and art the plank and bar of the abode of truth. Ere thou hadst knowledge to cry : ' My father ', and ' My mother ', thy Maker caused thee to delight in the fear of God. Thou hast prudent counsels, wherewith thou annoyest thine enemies and gladdenest the souls of thy friends. With the breath of thy mouth thou makest the foolish wise, and with thy pen's fluid washest off the blood of time's ignorance. Thou art like a cedar that grew high in wisdom's garden, so that the other shoots set forth their meditations unto thee. They are like an airy dream, like flying chaff, but thou renewest thy strength, and buddest by the glorious waters. Thy hand built for thee dominion with hewn stones, while other rulers plastered it with vanity. Thou art generous like thy fathers, and how pleasant it is to eat the second growth with grace, when the first is gone ! Thou turnest thy right hand's rivers as a honey stream, and makest them flow into the mouths of them that ask. Thou softenest thy generous heart toward the needy, but hardenest it like flint [4] against thy wealth. Thy soul urges thee to make the indigent rich, so that thou causest the name of poor to be forgotten. The sorrow-stricken man cheers up, on seeing thee : his wish is granted, when he calls thee by thy name.

[4] That is, *thou spendest money freely.*

Fain would I speak more of thee, but tempestuous is the sea of exile—who shall make its waves subside? I long to see the image of thy features in my dream, if only my pain allowed me to sleep! Thou art a garden of delights, but closed are its openings, that I should not smell the myrrh thereof. Time is thy slave, and yet it sends against me, day by day, the indignation and wrath of men. Hadst thou rebuked it, thou wouldest have pacified its wrath and its fierce anger, and it would have ceased to vex me.

My words have reached thee; command thou thy bounty that it should judge between me and between thy slave.[5] Here is the song, it is perfumed oil; take it, I pray, O man that art to be anointed with it now! A necklace! a word of glory on thy golden checker work, a speech on thy variegated chain.

3. Poem in Honor of the Wedding of Solomon b. Matir [6]

Is it a scent of myrrh, which pervades the air; or a breeze, which shakes the myrtles? A cloud, or a great mass of spicery? Lightning, or the sparkling of wine cups? Is it the clouds that pour out perfumes, or do the drops come from the myrtle tops? Is it the mouthless mountains that burst forth with joy, or doves and birds on boughs? The clothing of the earth is inwrought with gold, its coats are made of variegated silk. Its paths are straight to him that treads on them, and mountain-ridges have become like plains. The houses jubilantly shout, and the stone from the wall and the wooden beams respond. The erstwhile gloomy faces are now clad with joy, and

[5] That is, Time.
[6] Brody and Albrecht, *Sha'ar ha-Shir*, No. 59.

men of grief are merry and exult. The lips of stam-
merers now plainly speak, to build the house of mirth
that was destroyed. Indeed the mysterious wonders
now appear, that have been hidden in the heart of
time. The tent of glory has now been coupled, hooks
have been placed into the loops of praises. The days
have brought together bone to bone, and separated
bodies are now joined together. Upon the mounts of
myrrh have joys been set high, they are assembled on
the hills of frankincense.

On morning's wings a voice proclaims unto the
world (not on swift runners, nor on horses) : ' Solomon has lovingly betrothed a noble maid,' as though
the moon and sun had been betrothed.

Upon the path of prudence are his steps, his feet
walk and tread upon instruction. From early youth
his thoughts were on the skies, his meditations were
borne onto the constellations. He excels all men of his
own age, as sons of men excel all beasts and worms.
His deeds are far more precious than theirs, as rubies
are more precious than clay. They run to reach the
dust of his feet—how can a sparrow pursue the
hawks ?

Oh answer : how can Orion meet Pleiades on earth.
while none inquires, nor takes notice ? Is this not so ?
Are not their radiant wings spread upon their charming countenances ? How did they steal the light of the
stars ? Were men ever seen robbing and despoiling
heaven's lights ?

O all his friends, make haste to drink to-day the
wine of friendship in the bowls of joy. Be ready to
increase your merriment, and open ye the store-houses
of ease. The goblets are like frozen water, and the
burning coals have been dissolved in their midst. Drink

now as he appointed in his house; drink ye at your desire, without being forced.

O youth, rejoice in the lovely hind, and sing ye both in ecstasies of joy. Delight thou in a figure graceful as a palm-tree and lithe as the myrtle-twigs. Fear not the sound of her neck's ornaments, at twilight, nor the rustling of her veils. And be not terrified by dove-like eyes, drunk with the wine of passion's violence. Take courage, when embraced by arms bedecked with bracelets and with bangles of pure gold. Nor shouldst thou shun the snake-like locks that fall on a face bathed in maiden modesty; indeed, they come to thee in peace, though they conceal and hide the splendor of her face.[7]

And know that time is the slave of thy desire, assembled are its sons to do thy wish: they hasten to bring near what thou seekest, but drive away the sorrows of thy heart.

This song is from a friend whose heart rejoices in thee, whose thoughts fly and hasten to thee; it is a glorious robe which shall never grow old, till the foundations of the world are demolished. Indeed the water of his friendship is as pure as snow and is not fouled by feet; if in my heart it is concealed from thee, it is to be sought in the gardens of thy mind. For rubies are for men of intellect, while for the vain are fatlings of lambs; the brave men crave for words of eloquence, but fools hunger after fattened geese.

O noble scion, live at ease with the daughter of nobles, sheltered under the shadow of the Almighty!

[7] Four lines have been omitted in this translation.

XVIII JUDAH B. SAMUEL HA-LEVI

[Lucid thinker and melodious singer. Born at Toledo in the last quarter of the eleventh century, and died in the Orient in the middle of the twelfth. His philosophic work, written in Arabic, has always been a household word in Jewish homes in its Hebrew translation under the title *ha-Kozari*. His poems are the outburst of a deeply religious soul, and often describe his fervent love for Zion. Though under the influence of Arabic literature, his poems are more Jewish than those of the other great poets of that brilliant epoch.]

1. Ode to Zion [1]

O Zion, wilt thou not inquire about the peace of thy captives, they that seek thy peace and are the remnant of thy flocks? From west and east, from north and south, greetings from them that are far and near take thou on all sides. Greetings also from a slave of yearning, who sheds his tears like Hermon's dew, and longs that they fall on thy mounts.

I am like a jackal to bewail thy woe; but when I dream of thy restoration, I am a harp for thy songs. My heart moans for Bethel, and Peniel, and for Mahanaim, and all the meeting-places of thy pure ones. There God's Presence dwells near thee, and thy Creator opened thy gates toward the gates of heaven. The glory of the Lord alone was thy light; the sun, the moon, and stars illumined thee not.

I yearn that my soul be poured forth in the place where God's spirit was poured out on thy chosen ones. Thou art a royal house, thou art the throne of God, how then can bondmen sit upon the thrones of thy princes?

[1] Harkavy's edition, vol. I., p. 10; Bordy's edition, vol. II., p. 155.

Would that I were roaming about in the places where God appeared unto thy seers and messengers! Who would make me wings, that I may fly away? I would cause my broken heart to move amidst thy mounts of Bether! On thy ground fain would I lie prostrate; I would take pleasure in thy stones, and would love thy dust! Then standing by the sepulchres of my fathers, I would gaze with rapture on thy choicest graves in Hebron. I would pass through thy forest and Carmel, and stand in Gilead, and gaze with rapture on mount Abarim;—mount Abarim and mount Hor, where are thy two great luminaries, thy teachers who gave thee light.

Thine air is life for the souls, like myrrh are the grains of thy dust, and thy streams are like the honey-comb. It would be pleasant for me to walk naked and barefoot among thy desolate ruins, where once thy temples stood; where thy ark was hidden, and where thy Cherubim dwelled in thy innermost shrines.

I will pluck and cast away the beauty of my locks, and curse fate which defiled thy Nazirites in an unclean land. How can it be pleasant unto me to eat and drink, when I see that the curs drag thy young lions? or how can the light of the day be sweet to my sight, when I see the flesh of thine eagles in the mouth of ravens?

O cup of sorrow, gently! desist for a while! for my reins and soul are already filled with thy bitterness. When I remember Oholah, I drink thy poison; and when I remember Oholibah, I drain thy dregs.

O Zion, perfect of beauty, thou hast of yore combined love and grace, and the souls of thy companions are bound up with thee; they that rejoice in thy bliss, are grieved at thy desolation, and bewail thy misfortunes. From the pit of captivity they pant toward thee, and prostrate themselves, each from his place, toward thy gates; the flocks of thy multitude, that are exiled and scattered over mountain and hill, yet do not forget thy folds; that cling to thy skirts, and strive to go up and seize the boughs of thy palm-trees.

Can Shinar and Pathros in their greatness be likened to thee? can they compare their vanity to thy Truthfulness and Light?[2] Unto whom can they compare thy anointed and thy seers, unto whom thy Levites and thy singers? The crown of all vain kingdoms shall change and pass away, but thy strength is for ever, thy crowns are for all generations.

Thy God desired thee for His dwelling, and happy is the man whom He chooses and draws near to dwell in thy courts. Happy is he who waits, and will yet live to see the rising of thy light, when upon him shall thy dawns break forth, to behold the bliss of thy chosen ones, and to exult in thy joy, when the pristine glory of thy youth is restored to thee.

2. Meditations in Mid-Ocean [3]

Wilt thou at fifty still pursue childhood's folly, while thy days are ready to fly away? Wilt thou flee from the service of God, but eargerly serve men? wilt thou seek the multitude, but forsake the presence of the One who is sought in all affairs? Wilt thou neglect to make provision for thy journey, and sell thy portion for a pottage of lentils?

Unto thee thy soul has not yet said: ' Enough! ' but her lust bears new fruit each month; turn aside from her advice, and seek God's counsel; keep away

[2] That is, Thummim and Urim.
[3] Harkavy, vol. I., p. 28; Brody, vol. II., p. 160.

from the five senses. Reconcile thyself to thy Creator in the remainder of thy days which hurry and hasten. Seek not His good will with a double heart, and go not toward enchantments. Be strong as a leopard to do His will, swift as an antelope, and mighty as lions.

Let thy heart not fail in mid-ocean, when thou seest the mountains totter and move to and fro. Worn out are the hands of sailors, and skilful workers keep silence; they walk forward cheerfully, but they turn back, and are ashamed. The ocean is thy only refuge, there is no way to escape, the snares are all around.

The sails flutter and wave, the planks tremble and shake. The wind sports with the waters, like them that cast about the sheaves for threshing; for a while it flattens them like threshing-floors, and then it heaps them up like stacks. When the waves grow mighty, they are like lions; but when they subside, they seem like serpents; billow follows billow, fiercely chasing, like adders that will not be charmed.

The mighty vessel is well-nigh overthrown by a mighty breaker, and the mast and the riggings are loosened. The chambers of the ark are in confusion: no one knows which are the lower, the middle, or the upper ones. They that pull the riggings are in anguish, men and women are sorely grieved; troubled is the spirit of their captains—the bodies are weary of the souls. The strength of masts is of no avail, and the counsel of greybeards no longer pleases. Masts of cedar are counted like stubble, cypress-trees are turned into reeds. Weights of sand are like straw on the surface of the ocean, iron and stone are like chaff.

Then each man prays to his holiness, but thou turnest to the holy of the holies. Thou rememberest the

wonders of the Red Sea and the Jordan, which are
engraved on every heart. Thou then praisest Him
who stills the roaring of the ocean, when its waters
cast up mire. Thou mentionest to Him the iniquity
of unclean hearts, but He remembers for thee the
merit of the holy fathers. He renews His miracles,
when thou renewest before Him the song of the dancing of the Mahlites and Mushites.[4] He restores the
breath of life unto the bodies, and the dry bones live
again. In a moment the billows are stilled, and seem
like flocks scattered upon the face of the earth.

The night is (when the sun descends on the degrees,
and out comes the heavenly host with its captain) like
a Cushite woman whose clothing is inwrought with
gold, wrapt up in a diamond-spangled cloak of blue.
The stars are perplexed in mid-ocean, like strangers
driven out from their dwelling-places; they reflect
their light, in their likeness and their image, in the midst
of the sea, like flames and fires. The waters and the
sky are like brilliant and bright ornaments on the night.

The sea is like the heaven in appearance, they are
thus two encompassing seas; and between them is my
heart a third sea, when the billows of my new hymns
arise.

3. Letter Addressed to Nathan b. Samuel[5]

To the store-house of understanding and stronghold
of faith, the crown of the scholars and chief of the
speakers, the pride of the Torah and the bowl of the
candlestick, our master and teacher Rabbi Nathan the

---

[4] Levitic families; comp. Exodus 6. 19.
[5] Harkavy, vol. I., p. 158; Brody, vol. I., p. 214. It is written
in rhymed prose, and is an excellent specimen of the rhetorical
and florid style in which the Arabs and their Jewish imitators
delighted.

scholar, son of the glory of the greatness of the holiness of our master and teacher Rabbi Samuel the scholar, of blessed memory, from one who bows himself down before him and longs to behold his countenance, Judah the Levite, son of Rabbi Samuel (may his soul be in paradise!).

Stones of the crown lifted on high, glorying in the crown of our generation, deriving their genealogy from the Foundation Stone, and mocking every other precious stone! Thou art the crown that is set upon the stone of salvation; all thy border is of desirable stones: the chief stone is above thee, graceful stones are at thy right and at thy left, and thou hast rays coming forth from thy hand. I shall divide the seas, and stir up the shades, for I shall arouse myself to sing, when Nathan the prophet comes to me. The meditations of my heart are in commotion, and my thoughts impel me to write. Thou didst humble me, yet didst thou delight me, for thou didst lead me with honor, though with heaviness, and put upon me the crown and the testimony. Thou didst robe me with thy raiment, attire me with thy mitres, and strengthen me with thy power. But who can don thy crowns, and who can put on thy wreaths? Gates of justice are thy gates, lofty mountains are thy mountains, and twilights of desire are thy dawns. When thou devisest a law, thou causest the advice of others to fail; when thou counsellest, thou breakest every rod; every mouth becomes dumb, even the eloquent feels ashamed, and they who compose songs have mouths, but speak not: their fountains are stopped up, and they themselves are still as a stone in the presence of a fountain whose waters fail not. Thy heavens do not become black, and thy rains are not withheld. Thy store-houses are filled, and thy spices send forth their fragrance. The manna descends upon him that hearkens to thy words. Wonderful are thy words, and thy compositions are awe-inspiring; they fly to the west and to the south, and speak from on high. Shall Egypt detain such a man, while Jerusalem, as well as the land of Merathaim,[6] longs for thee? Thou art a bundle of myrrh held in the hands and sought betwixt the breasts; thy fame tells concerning thee and likewise about thy thoughts. The mixtures of thy perfumes proclaim before thee: ' Bow the knee '; and thy books reveal thy secrets. Thy name gave [7] forth thy taste and thy pleasant dainties; the wonderful sage, the exalted crown; yea, thy name is greater than all; our master and teacher, Nathan the scholar, the crown of scholars, the son of the glory of our master and teacher Samuel the scholar, the righteous, of blessed memory. From one who is a portion of thy lights and a tributary of thy rivers, Judah the Levite, thy disciple, the gleaning of thy harvest, and the fallen fruit of thy vintage; who sends his heart ahead of his writings; who is fearful and faint-hearted to consider his affairs. Shall I prosper when I come forth with my ploughshare and coulter to meet the Cherethite and Pelethite, a mighty nation that arranges battle-lines like Benaiah and Ethan? Who am I, what is my life, and what is my desire and wish? Worthless dust, crushed and ill; fearful on account of my iniquity and the sins of my youth and old age. Yet I ventured to stand upon thy thresholds with my supplications, though I am but a wayfarer that turns aside to tarry for a night, a Levite who sojourns there. Wherewith shall I draw

---

[6] That is, Babylon.
[7] In the original this word represents also Nathan.

nigh, and how shall I vie with the ruler and potentate?
I summoned counsels from afar, took up my weapons,
came in, and went out; but I found nothing better than
silence. I was humiliated, and put to shame, and despaired of an answer; I lost heart to come out to meet
thee; I groped for the wall in the dark, and felt my
way like the blind, and sought hiding-places, until I
met taskmasters, who were urgent, persistent, and
pressing; they came from the wonderful sage, the
lord, the exalted nobleman, our master and teacher
Halfon the Levite, who speaks in thy name, and en-
deavors to take hold of thee, O my lord and my pride,
may he be exalted and lifted up, and may he be very
high. He stands between us to join our hearts with the
exchange of our writings and the purity of our love.
He importuned me, pressed me, urged me, aroused me,
and brought me out hastily from the dungeon of slothfulness. He coaxed me, without restraining himself,
saying: ' Come now, I will prove thee; finish thy work,
and give the best thereof which is full of understanding; perform at thy old age the deeds of youth. Know
before whom thou art about to render the account,
near whom thou writest, and near whom thou signest.'
Thy enchanters hurried, and thy magicians did great
things, until they annulled my vows, and made my
bonds void. Then my bands dropped off, my youth was
renewed, my songs thronged tumultuously, my lyres
were sounded, and forgotten were my fears and the
years of the life of my sojournings. I remembered not
that the day declined toward evening, that the eternal
lodging-place was near by, while there was yet abundant work. I mingled with the throng, aroused myself with youth, eagerly sought the dawn of life, and
dissembled hoariness, as one dissembles a stolen thing,

8

though my leanness testified against me. Then I took some of thy words, and with wrestlings did I wrestle with the lion, and prevailed; I rescued a piece of an ear, and made merry with myself, for I was likened to the scribes of the king and to them that have ability to stand in the king's palace. My lord, in thy kindness pardon thy servant, and be not too exacting with me, and weigh not my words; judge me in the scale of merit, and bring me not into the judgment of thy wisdom. Behold, here is the fruit of my intellect, the choicest of my musing, and the best of my meditations, according to the ability of my hand and tongue, until I come unto my lord to watch at thy doors, to gather thy pearls, and to sing thy praises. Lo, these are but the outskirts of thy paths, and a little of the splendor of thy moons. He that makes peace in His high places shall increase thy peace, shall make thy friends perfect, shall fight against thine enemies, and establish thy plans, that thou mayest spend thy days in prosperity. I conclude with peace. Amen.

XIX. ABRAHAM B. MEIR IBN EZRA

[Poet, philologist, and astronomer. He was born in Spain about 1092, and died in 1167. He acquired great fame as grammarian and biblical exegete, as poet, and as astronomer. The greater bulk of his poems are liturgic; but he also has a number of fine secular poems. His commentaries are based on sound principles of exegesis, and his poems are replete with deep feeling.]

1. Plaintive Song [1]

Where is thy might, O right hand of the Lord?—I heard of thee by the hearing of the ear;—but now I have despaired of lifting up my head, as though I had never known of thee.

The fire of jealousy burns within me for the queen that now languishes in bonds; she is the derision and scorn of all creatures, bound to a life-long widowhood. My foes are prosperous and at rest, but I am an exile, and wander to and fro.

The hand of the polluter rules over me, and he taunts me: 'I am holier than thou; how canst thou hope, while generations have passed, and thou art still in my bondage?'

Enough have I been sitting in the dark, pondering with grief on my misfortune; how can I hope to find a cure for me, while my God dwells not in my midst? I weep for my soul, and how shall I give respite to my heart?

Ask, O city of Ariel, ask if I have ever forgotten thee; tears flow like rivers from mine eyes, for I left thee without glory.

[1] Egers' edition, p. 50. This poem is complicated in its structure. It consists of seven stanzas, and the initial letters of stanzas 1, 2, 4, and 6 are the author's name אברם.

In visions of appointed seers I meet not the end of
my captivity; and I seek among all the prophets, but
I know not the mystery of my redemption. My
trespasses have caused me grief; yet I heard a voice
which gladdened me. Each prophet said to my inheritance: 'How can I abandon thee? Because of the
affection of the days of youth I bear for thee an everlasting love.'

2. Penitential Prayer [2]

I prostrate myself with my face to the ground, since
nothing lower exists; I humbly cast myself down before the Most High, who is the highest of all high.

O, wherewith shall I meet His countenance? if with
my spirit, comes it not from Him? if with my choicest
flesh? He gave it life, and man has nought that is
nobler than his soul! There is no end and no beginning to His greatness—how can my tongue extol Him?
Much farther is He than the heavens of the heavens,
yet near to my flesh and bone.

Behold, I come to Thee, my God, because there is
none besides Thee that can benefit. Have not all the
hosts of heaven and of earth like me been created by
Thy hand? How shall I then seek help from them?
is not the help of all created things in vain? A slave
can flee to none for refuge, but unto his master who
acquired him.

Why should I expect to know aught, knowing that
Thou hast created me for my good? Thy lovingkindnesses are more than can be told, but my sins ex-
ceed the sand. How shall I lift up mine eye unto
Thee, since mine eye also has grievously transgressed?

---

[2] Egers, p. 147. It consists of twenty lines without rhymes.
The double acrostic reads אברהם מעזרה.

What more shall my lips utter in response, since also they have dealt very wickedly? The wantonness of my heart did unto me that which my adversary could not do. Hot wrath has overtaken me because of that; woe unto me, for I rebelled! My evil inclination led me astray, for I desired not to provoke Thee. My evils harmed only me, but Thou alone wilt show me lovingkindness. Make known to me a way to profit me, for Thou didst teach me all that I know. I caused the prayers of my heart to be heard by mine ears; mayest Thou hear them in heaven!

3. The Epistle of Hai b. Mekiz [3]

Hear, O wise men, my words, and ye that have knowledge, give ear unto me; consider, O noble men and greybeards, and hearken, ye that are ignorant and young; for my mouth shall utter truth, and the opening of my lips shall be right things. I have left my house, forsaken my inheritance, and abandoned my place, the land of my birth, and my people, because my mother's sons were incensed against me, and made me keeper of a vineyard which is not mine own. I therefore betook myself to travel and to seek repose, so that my spirit and soul may find rest and have respite, and my life may be in solitude. With me were companions who hearkened unto my words. And behold, there was an old man walking in the field, praising and rendering thanks to God. His likeness was as the likeness of kings, and his majesty was as the majesty of angels. Time changed him not,

[3] Egers, p. 139; Rosin, I, p. 168. This is the first part of this composition which is in rhymed prose. The author meets Hai b. Mekiz (the Living, Son of the Wakeful), who urges him to leave his companions and to seek wisdom.

nor did the years alter him. His eyes were as the
eyes of doves, and his temples as a piece of a pome-
granate. His stature was not bent, nor did his strength
fail. His eye was not dim, nor his natural force
abated. His oils were as fragrant as the odor of
spikenard plants. His mouth was most sweet, yea, he
was altogether lovely. I said unto him: ' May peace
be multiplied unto thee, and mayst thou never go
astray! Whose son art thou? what is thy name?
what is thine occupation? and which is thy place?'

And he answered me with words set with precious
stones and with speeches arranged as the Thummim
and Urim. And he said unto me: ' May God make
thy name good, and may thy peace be as a river. May
He continually be thy confidence, and keep thy foot
from being taken! My name is Hai b. Mekiz, and
the holy city is my place, and my occupation is that
in which thou seest me engaged without being
wearied: I run to and fro in every city and province,
in every nook and corner. My father led me in the
way of wisdom, and taught me knowledge and discretion. I was with him a nursling in Baal-hamon*;
in his shadow I sat down with great delight and
did not move, for his fruit was sweet to my taste.'

And it came to pass, when we talked, and the
speeches were extended (they were all plain to him
that understands, and right to him that finds knowledge), that he said unto me: ' The show of thy countenance tells, and thy face testifies that thine ears
are open to hear instructions, and that thy soul is
prepared to acquire wisdom and understanding. Now
this work which I examine and investigate never fails,

* That is, the multitude, crowd.

nor deceives, for it is like balances to truth, and like eyes to the seer; he who neglects it shall grope at noonday. But these friends who have dominion over thee are not friends, but banish thee; they are not comrades, but do evil unto thee; they are not lovers, but enemies; they spread and hide snares and nets, and imprison and afflict the valiant and the mighty. Happy is he who is delivered from them, but the sinner shall be caught by them; he who is ensnared in their net shall not be saved, and he who is caught in their snare shall not escape. O my son, depart from their tents, and turn not unto them, nor hearken unto their words, because their feet run to evil. The one who walks before thee [5] multiplies falsehood, and casts truth away. The other at thy right hand [6] humbles and afflicts thee; he is angry and wroth at all times, and is indignant and vexatious every day; his swords strike them that are near him, and his sparks consume all around him; his anger burns as a fire, and his wrath rages as a flame; he is erring and foolish in everything, and swerves and deviates from truth; he is like a lion that longs to tear, and like a young lion that lurks in secret places to snatch. The one at thy left hand [7] causes thee to stumble, and consumes thee; he ever waits and hopes, and continually covets and desires; even if thou shouldst bray him in a mortar, his foolishness will not depart from him, and even if thou shouldst smite him with a hammer, his folly will not cease; he loves all food, and cannot have enough of gifts. Now he who is in their midst does not understand, and has no wisdom; he

[5] That is, Imagination.
[6] That is, Emotions, Passions, and Moods.
[7] That is, Lust and Appetite.

speaks falsehood, and utters vanity; he perverts justice, and corrupts truth; perverseness is in his heart,
and he devises iniquity upon his bed; his eye is not
satisfied with seeing, nor his ear filled with hearing.
Yet thou followest them closely, and thy heart loves
and desires them; but thou knowest not that he who
walks in their paths will not be delivered from their
destructions.   Can a man take fire in his bosom, and
his clothes not be burned? or can one walk upon hot
coals, and his feet not be scorched? so is he that is made
to yield by the flattering of their mouth, and he that
is allured by the sweetness of their words.   My son,
walk thou not in the way with them, refrain thy foot
from their path; for they have cast down many
wounded, and laid low mighty and valiant men.   Their
way and their paths are the ways to Sheol, and the
tracks to death are their tracks and highways.   Rule
thou over them, and control them; humble the foolish
among them with the aid of the lustful, and the lustful with the aid of the foolish.   Judge them in righteousness, and pervert not justice.   As for him among
them who speaks vanity and falsehood, thou shalt not
consent unto him, nor hearken unto him; even when
he speaks fair, believe him not, for seven abominations
are in his heart.   Do this now, my son, and deliver
thyself, before the day breathes and the shadow flees
away: Heed my words, and forget them not, nor
shouldst thou ever forsake them; keep them continually
in thy bosom, and write them upon the tablet of thy
heart; let them be for thyself alone, and not for
strangers beside thee.   For they shall be chaplets of
grace unto thy head, and chains about thy neck, so
that thy days may be spent in prosperity, and thy
years in pleasantness.'

And it came to pass, when I heard from him these words, which are more precious than rubies (and I knew that he who departs from his instructions and changes his sayings, or causes aught of his words to fall, wrongs and destroys his soul, and harms and kills his spirit, while he who takes fast hold of them, and lets them not go, shall live for ever, and shall not be destroyed; for they are life unto those that find them, and health to all their flesh), that I said: ' Draw me, I shall run after thee. I shall rejoice and exult in thee; and shall be more glad and joyous with thy love than with spiced wine and sweet juice.'

And he said unto me: ' Thou art not able to run at my side, nor to fly with me, for thy wings are broken, and thou hast no pinions.'

Then I said: ' Oh that I had wings like a dove! then would I fly away, and be at rest! I pray thee, my lord, look not unto my presumtuousness, for unto thee have I revealed my cause, and upon thee have I cast my burden. In thee is my hope and expectation; cure thou my sickness, and bind up my wound.'

So he led me through a short way to a spacious land, which is divided into three parts that are deep and distant. The beginning of one is in the water, and its end is in heaven. As for the remaining two, which are the chief parts, one ends in the east, and the other begins in the west. They give each other light, and clothe each other with splendor. These parts form the chief divisions of the land. None is able to walk in these lofty places, except a man filled with the spirit of God. At the end of this land there is a murmuring spring, which makes its voice heard at a distance. Its streams are rivers, and its waters are mighty waters; they heal every wound and disease, and produce heal-

ing and medicine. When we approached and stood
near it, he stripped me of my coat, which he cast
away, and brought me down naked into the midst of
the spring, and he said unto me: 'Drink waters out
of its fountain, and running waters out of its well;
for through it shall thy wounds be bound up, and thy
pinions shall be healed; and thou shalt have wings to
soar in the heavens.'

Then I drank of the waters of life, which quicken
the souls; and my agonies and plagues and sore
and steadfast sicknesses departed from me. The waters
were unto me like balsam to heal my wound and my
pinion. I drank as much as was sufficient for me, and
was cured of my sickness.

XX. ABRAHAM IBN DAUD

[Spanish philosopher, historian, and astronomer. He was born at Toledo about 1110, and died as a martyr in 1180. His best known books are his philosophic work, written in Arabic and entitled *al-'Akidah al-Rafi'ah* (The Sublime Faith), which has only been preserved in a Hebrew translation, and his *Book of Tradition,* which was written in 1161.]

The Four Captives [1]

After Hezekiah, who was head of the academy and exilarch, the academies and the Geonim ceased to exist. But prior to that it was brought about by the Holy One, blessed be He, that the income of the academies which used to come to them from the land of Spain, the land of Maghrib, Africa, Egypt, and Palestine, should be discontinued. The incident was brought about in the following manner: There came forth from the city of Cordova a captain appointed over a fleet, whose name was Ibn Damahin, and who was sent by the Ishmaelitish king of Spain, whose name was 'Abd al-Rahman. This commander of mighty ships went forth to conquer the ships of Edom and the towns that were close to the sea-shore. They reached as far as the coast of Palestine, turned around to the Greek Archipelago and the islands thereof, and met a boat which carried four great sages travelling from the city of Bari to a city called Safsatin. These sages were travelling to collect money for the academy. Ibn Damahin captured the boat, and took the sages captive. One of these sages was Rabbi Hushiel, father

[1] Neubauer, *Mediæval Jewish Chronicles,* vol. I., pp. 67, *seq.*

of Rabbenu Hananel; the second was Rabbi Moses,
father of Rabbi Enoch (he was taken captive together
with his wife and Rabbi Enoch his son; Rabbi Enoch
was then a young lad) ; the third was Rabbi Shemariah
the son of Rabbi Elhanan; as for the fourth, his name
is unknown to me.   When the captain wanted to force
the wife of Rabbi Moses and to humble her, because
she was exceedingly beautiful and well favored, she
cried out to Rabbi Moses her husband in the holy
tongue, and asked him whether they that were
drowned in the sea would be quickened at the time
of the resurrection of the dead, or not.   He replied
unto her: ' The Lord said: " I will bring again from
Bashan, I will bring them again from the depths of
the sea." ' ²   When she heard him say that they would
be quickened, she threw herself into the sea, so that
she sank and died.

These sages did not say anything about themselves
or their wisdom.   The captain sold Rabbi Shemariah
in Alexandria of Egypt; the latter went up to Cairo,
where he became head of a school; Rabbi Hushiel
was sold on the coast of Africa, whence he went up
to the city of Kairuwan, which in those days was the
mightiest of all Ishmaelitish cities in the land of
Maghrib.   There Rabbi Hushiel became head of a
school, and there he begot Rabbi Hananel his son.
Then the captain went to Cordova, where he sold
Rabbi Moses and Rabbi Enoch his son.   They were
redeemed by the men of Cordova, who were not aware
of the great learning of the captives.

There was in Cordova a synagogue that was called
the Synagogue of the House of Study, and there was
a judge named Rabbi Nathan, who was exceedingly

² Psalm 68. 23.

pious. The people of Spain, however, were not well-versed in the words of our teachers of blessed memory. Nevertheless, with the little knowledge that they possessed, they arranged discussions, interpretations, and arguments. Once Rabbi Nathan the judge interpreted the law that an ablution is required for each sprinkling, which occurs in the tractate Yoma, and they were not able to explain it. Whereupon Rabbi Moses, who sat in a corner like a beadle, stood up before Rabbi Nathan, and said to him : ' My master, there would be too many ablutions.' When he and his pupils heard his words, they marvelled one with the other, and asked him to explain the law to them ; whereupon he explained the law in the right manner. They then asked him to explain all their difficulties, and they set forth their questions, which he answered with the abundance of his wisdom. There were litigants outside the House of Study who were not permitted to enter until the pupils had finished their lesson. On that day Rabbi Nathan the judge came out, and the litigants went after him. But he said to them : ' I am no longer judge ; but this man, who is clad in sackcloth and is a stranger, is my teacher and master, and I am his pupil from to-day and henceforth. Now appoint ye him judge in the congregation of Cordova.' And they did so. The congregation gave him a good allowance, and presented him with costly garments and a carriage.

The captain then wanted to cancel his sale, but the king would not permit him, for he rejoiced with great joy when he heard that the Jews of his kingdom no longer needed the men of Babylon.

When the report thereof was heard in all the land of Spain and the land Maghrib, all the pupils came to study under Rabbi Moses, and all the questions that formerly had been addressed to the academies were directed to him.

This took place in the days of Sherira Gaon, approximately about the year four thousand seven hundred and fifty.

Rabbi Moses allied himself by marriage with the children of Palyaj, that family being the most prominent of all the families of the Cordova community; and he took from among them a wife for Rabbi Enoch his son, and a daughter of Rabbi Enoch was married to one of the children of Palyaj. This name is, therefore, still found among the children of Palyaj until this day.

Rabbi Moses had numerous pupils, one of whom was Rabbi Joseph the son of Rabbi Isaac Ibn Satnas, known as Ibn Abitor, who explained the entire Talmud in Arabic to the Ishmaelitish king whose name was al-Hakim.

XXI. BENJAMIN OF TUDELA

[A famous traveller of the twelfth century. He seems to have been a merchant in Spain. He travelled for about thirteen years (1160-1173). He very vividly and graphically described everything he saw, and his book contains interesting details about the various Jewish communities of the twelfth century.]

Description of Jerusalem and Its Surroundings [1]

From there it is three parasangs to Jerusalem, which is a small city, fortified by three walls. There are many people in it, and the Ishmaelites call them Jacobites, Arameans, Greeks, Georgians, Franks, and peoples of all other tongues. There is a dyeing-house there, which the Jews rent annually from the king on condition that nobody beside the Jews should be engaged in dyeing in Jerusalem. There are about two hundred Jews dwelling under the tower of David, in one corner of the city. The first structure of the foundation of the wall of the tower of David, to the extent of ten cubits, is part of the ancient structure which our ancestors set up, but the remaining portion was built by the Ishmaelites. There is no structure in the whole city stronger than the tower of David.

The city contains also two buildings, one being a hospital, from which four hundred knights issue forth, and where all the sick that come thither are lodged and receive all their needs in life and in death. The second building is called the Temple of Solomon; it is the palace which was built by Solomon king of

[1] Asher, *The Itinerary of Rabbi Benjamin of Tudela*, pp. 34, seq.; M. Adler's edition, pp. כ״ג, seq.

Israel, peace be upon him. Knights are quartered
there, three hundred of whom issue forth every day
for military exercises, besides the knights that come
from the land of the Franks and from the land of
Edom, having taken a vow upon themselves to serve
there a year or two until their vow is fulfilled. In that
city is the great place of worship called the Sepulchre;
there is the burial-place of that man,[2] to which all the
misguided repair.

There are four gates in Jerusalem: the gate of
Abram, the gate of David, the gate of Zion, and the
gate of Goshafat, which is the gate of Jehoshaphat,
in front of the sanctuary which stood there in ancient
times. There is also the *Templum Domini,* which is
on the site of the temple, upon which ' Omar the
son of al-Khattab erected a very large and magnificent
cupola. The Gentiles are not allowed to introduce
there any image or effigy; they only come there to
pray. In front of that place is the Western Wall
which is one of the walls of the holy of holies. This
is called the Gate of Mercy, and thither all the Jews
repair to pray in front of the wall of the temple court.

There, in Jerusalem, attached to the house which
belonged to Solomon, are horse-stalls which he built;
it is a very strong structure, built of immense stones;
the like of this building was not seen in all the world.
There is still to be seen to-day the pool where the
priests used to slaughter their sacrifices, and the people
coming thither from Judah used to inscribe their names
upon the wall. A man going out through the gate of
Jehoshaphat would arrive at the valley of Jehoshaphat,
which is the wilderness of the nations. There is the

[2] That is, Christ.

pillar of Absalom's Monument, and the grave of king Uzziah. There is likewise a great fountain, and the waters of Shiloah flowing into the brook of Kidron. Over the spring there is a large structure, dating back from the days of our ancestors. Little water is found there, and most of the people of Jerusalem drink rain-water, for they have cisterns in their houses.

From the valley of Jehoshaphat one ascends the mount of Olives, as only this valley intervenes between Jerusalem and the mount of Olives. From the mount of Olives one can see the Sea of Sodom (it is two parasangs from the Sea of Sodom to the Pillar of Salt into which Lot's wife turned; the sheep lick it, but it afterwards regains its original shape), and the whole land of the plain and the valley of Shittim as far as mount Nebo.

In front of Jerusalem is mount Zion; but there is no building on mount Zion, except a place of worship belonging to the uncircumcised.

About three miles before Jerusalem are the sepul-chres of the Israelites, for they used to bury their dead in caves in those days. Each sepulchre bears a date; but the children of Edom demolish the sepul-chres, and of the stones thereof they build their houses. These sepulchres reach as far as the border of Ben-jamin at Zelzah.

Around Jerusalem there are great mountains, and on mount Zion are the sepulchres of the house of David, and the sepulchres of the kings who arose after him. The place, however, is no longer known, on account of the following incident. Fifteen years ago part of the place of worship, which is on mount Zion, fell in, and the patriarch said to his overseer: ' Take the stones from the old walls, and restore the place

9

of worship with them.' The latter did so, and hired workmen; twenty men, at fixed wages, were pulling out the stones from the foundation of the wall of Zion. Among these men were two very intimate friends. One day one of them made a banquet for his friend. After the meal they returned to their work, and their overseer said to them: 'Wherefore have ye come late to-day?' They answered and said: 'Wherefore dost thou chide us? When our fellow-workmen go to their meal, we will do our work.' When meal-time came, and the other workmen went to their meal, these two continued to pull out stones. They raised a certain stone, and found the mouth of a cave beneath it. Thereupon one said to his friend: 'Let us go in and see whether there is any money in there.' Having passed through the entrance of the cave, they reached a large hall supported by pillars of marble overlaid with silver and gold. In front was a table of gold and a sceptre and crown. This was the sepulchre of king David. At the left thereof was the sepulchre of king Solomon in like fashion, and so were the sepulchres of the kings of Judah that were buried there. Closed coffers were also there, and no man knows what they contain. When these two men wanted to enter the hall, a stormy wind came forth from the entrance of the cave, and smote them, so that they fell like dead to the ground. They lay there until evening, when another wind came forth, crying out as if with a man's voice: 'Arise and go forth from this place!' The men went out from there in haste and terror, and came to the patriarch, and related these things to him. The patriarch then sent for Rabbi Abraham al-Constantini, the pious ascetic, who was one of the mourners for Jerusalem, and he related

all these things to him according to the narrative of
the two men who had come out from there. And
Rabbi Abraham answered, and said to him: ‘These
are the sepulchres of the house of David, that is, of
the kings of Judah; and to-morrow I and thou and
these men shall go in and see what is there.’ On the
following day they sent for the two men and found
them lying in their beds. Filled with terror, the
men said: ‘We will not enter there, for God desires
not to show it to any man.’ The patriarch then commanded them to close up that place and to keep it concealed from men unto this day. The afore-mentioned
Rabbi Abraham related these things to me.

XXII. THE BOOK OF YASHAR

[A collection of legends concerning biblical heroes. It is also known under the titles of *Toledot Adam* and *Dibre ha-Yamin ha-Arok*. It had been assumed that this was the Book of Jashar mentioned in Joshua 10.13, and elsewhere. But this assumption was long ago given up by all scholars. In all likelihood this book originated in southern Italy during the twelfth century. The style is a good imitation of the narrative books of the Bible.]

Moses Having Taken a Besieged City Is Proclaimed King of Cush [1]

So Moses reigned on that day over all the children of Cush instead of Kikanus king of Cush. In the fifty-fifth year of the reign of Pharaoh king of Egypt, that is, in the hundred and fifty-seventh year after the children of Israel went down into Egypt, did Moses reign over Cush. Twenty-seven years old was Moses when he began to reign over Cush, and forty years did he reign. And the Lord made Moses find grace and favor in the sight of the children of Cush, and the children of Cush loved him exceedingly. And Moses was good with the Lord and with men.

And it came to pass on the seventh day of his reign that all the children of Cush gathered together. And they all met together, and came before Moses, and bowed down to him to the ground. And all the children of Cush together spoke to the king, saying: ' Give us counsel, that we may see what is to be done to this city. For it is to-day nine years that we are besieging this city, and we have not seen our children and our wives.'

[1] *Sefer ha-Yashar* on Exodus, Venice edition, pp. 135a, *seq.*

And the king answered them, saying: ' If ye will
hearken to my voice in all that I shall command you,
then the Lord will deliver the city into our hands, and
we shall take it. For if we fight against them as in
the first battle which we fought before king Kikanus
died, many of us shall fall down slain, as before.
Now, behold, here is counsel for you in this matter:
if ye will hearken to my voice, the city will be delivered into our hands.'

And all the armies answered the king, saying: ' All
that which our lord commands us will thy servants do.'

So Moses said unto them: ' Pass through, and proclaim in the whole camp, unto all the people, saying:
Thus says the king: Go into the forest, and bring of
the young of the stork, each man a young one in his
hand. And whosoever will transgress the command
of the king, and will not bring his young one, shall be
put to death, and the king shall take away all his
belongings. And it shall come to pass that, when ye
bring them, they shall be in your keeping, and ye
shall rear them until they grow up, and ye shall teach
them to swoop, in the manner of the young of the
hawk.'

And the children of Cush hearkened to the words
of Moses, and they arose, and caused it to be proclaimed throughout the camp, saying: ' Unto you, all
the children of Cush, is the king's command: Go
ye all together into the forest, and take for you of
the young of the stork, each man his young one in
his hand, and ye shall bring them with you. Now
whosoever shall rebel against the command of the
king, shall be put to death, and the king shall take
away all his belongings.'

So the people did according to his command; and
they went to the forest, and climbed up the fir-trees,
and they took, each man his young one in his hand,
all the young of the stork, and they brought them
with them in the evening. And they reared them according to the command of the king, and they taught
them to swoop like the young of the hawk; according to all that the king commanded them, so did all
the children of Cush.

And it came to pass that, when the young of the
stork grew up, the king commanded to let them hunger for three days. And all the people did so.

And it came to pass on the third day that the king
said unto them: ' Strengthen yourselves and be men
of valor; and put on every man his armor, and gird
on every man his sword upon him, and ride every man
his horse, and take every man his young of the stork
in his hand. And we shall rise up, and fight against
the city from the place where the serpents are.' And
all the people did according to the command of the
king, and every man took his young of the stork in
his hand, and they went forth.

And it came to pass, when they reached the place of
the serpents, that the king said unto them: ' Send
forth every man his young stork upon the serpents.'
So every man sent forth his young stork, according
to the command of the king. And the young storks
swooped upon the serpents, and devoured them all,
and destroyed them out of that place. And when the
people and the king saw that all the serpents were
destroyed out of that place, all the people shouted
with a great shout. And they drew nigh, and fought
against the city, and they seized upon it and took it;
and they entered the city. And there died on that

day of the people of the city one thousand and a hundred men, all the inhabitants of the city. But of the people who were besieging not one died. Then all the children of Cush went every man to his house, and to his wife, and to his children, and to all that he possessed.

Now when Balaam the soothsayer saw that the city was taken, he opened the gate, and he and his two sons and eight brothers fled; and they returned to Egypt, to Pharoah king of Egypt. They are the sorcerers and magicians mentioned in the Book of the Law, who stood against Moses when the Lord brought all the plagues upon Egypt.

So Moses took the city by his wisdom, and the children of Cush set him on the throne of the kingdom, instead of Kikanus king of Cush. And they set the royal crown on his head, and gave him queen Adonijah the Cushite, the wife of Kikanus, to wife. But Moses feared the Lord, the God of his fathers, and he went not in unto her, nor did he turn his eyes to her. For Moses remembered how Abraham had made Eliezer his servant swear, saying: ' Take not a wife for my son Isaac of the daughters of Canaan ' [2]; and also that which Isaac had done, when Jacob fled from before his brother, how he commanded him, saying: ' Take not a wife of the daughters of Canaan, nor shalt thou make marriages with any of the children of Ham; for the Lord our God gave Ham the son of Noah and all his seed as servants unto the children of Shem and unto the children of Japheth, and unto their seed after them for ever.' [3] Therefore

[2] Comp. Genesis 24. 3. The verse is not quoted verbatim.
[3] Comp. *ibid*. 28. 1. The verse is amplified. See also *ibid*. 9. 26, 27.

Moses turned not his heart nor his eyes to the wife of Kikanus all the days that he reigned over Cush.

And Moses feared the Lord, the God of his fathers, all his days. And Moses walked before the Lord in truth, with all his heart, and with all his soul; Moses departed not from the good way all the days of his life; he turned not to the right hand nor to the left from the way in which Abraham, Isaac, and Jacob had walked. And Moses strengthened himself in the kingdom of the children of Cush, and he guided the children of Cush in justice by his wisdom. And Moses prospered in his kingdom.

XXIII. JUDAH B. SAUL IBN TIBBON

[A famous translator of Arabic books into Hebrew. He was born at Granada in 1120, and died towards the end of the twelfth century. He did a great deal for the development of the Hebrew language, having practically created or at least systematized the philosophic terms. It is due to his efforts and to those of his fellow-workers, the best of whom were his descendants, that the philosophic literature of the Jews has reached the readers for whom it was intended. He translated the works of Sa'adya, Ibn Janah, Ibn Gebirol, and Judah ha-Levi.]

Why the Jewish Religion Does Not Especially Encourage Asceticism [1]

Said the Khazarite: Thou hast explained, O Rabbi, and drawn a comparison; indeed thou wast skilful in thy explanation and comparison. But we should expect to see more hermits and ascetics among you than among other nations.

Said the Rabbi: I regret very much that thou hast forgotten the principles which I previously expounded to thee and the truth of which thou didst admit. Did we not agree that it is impossible for any man to draw near to God except by means of deeds commanded by God? Dost thou think that this drawing near to God is only to be meek and humble, and the like?

Said the Khazarite: It is so in truth, and so do I think; I also read in your books as follows: 'What doth the Lord thy God require of thee, but to fear the Lord thy God?' [2] and another verse says: 'What

[1] Judah ha-Levi's *Book of the Khazarite,* part II, 45-50. Hirschfeld's edition, pp. 107, *seq.*
[2] Deuteronomy 10. 12.

137

doth the Lord require of thee, but to do justly, and to love mercy?'[3] and many other passages.

Said the Rabbi: These and similar things are the rational laws, which are the preambles and bases of the divine Law, preceding it in character and time, and without which the administration of any human society is impossible. Even a band of robbers must adopt a standard of justice among them, otherwise their confederacy would not last. When the disobedience of the children of Israel had come to such a pass that they disregarded the rational and social laws (without which no society can exist, just as no individual can exist without the natural functions like eating, drinking, movement, rest, sleeping, and waking), but nevertheless held fast to ceremonial worship, like sacrifices and other divine laws that were prescribed to them, He was satisfied with even less. He said: 'Would that ye observed those laws which even the meanest community observes, as the adoption of justice, the right path, and the acknowledgment of the Creator's bounty!' For the divine laws are not complete until the social and rational laws become perfected, and the rational laws include the adoption of justice and the acknowledgment of the Creator's bounty. Now how can he, who does not cling to these laws, adhere to sacrifices, Sabbath, circumcision, and other ceremonies, which reason neither necessitates, nor rejects? But these are the very laws which were especially given to the children of Israel in addition to the rational ones, and it is through them that they received the advantage of the divine influence, though they knew not why these laws were necessary, just as they knew not how the glory of God descended

[3] Micah 6. 8.

upon them, or the fire of God upon their sacrifices; or how they heard the speech of God; or how all the other things occurred to them. Reason would not accept these matters, if not for the irrefutable testimony of by-standers and eye-witnesses. In a similar manner it was said unto them: 'What doth the Lord require of thee?'[4], and 'Add your burnt-offerings unto your sacrifices'[5], and other verses of a similar nature. Is it possible that an Israelite, confining himself to the doing of justice and the loving of kindness, while forsaking circumcision, Sabbath, and the laws of Passover and other laws, would prosper?

Said the Khazarite: Not in accordance with that which thou hast said before; but in the opinion of the philosophers he would be a pious man, even if he does not care by which religion he draws near to God, whether by becoming a Jew or a Christian, or by a religion which he devises for himself. Now we have returned to analogy, reasoning, and dialectics. Accordingly, every man would endeavor to establish that law to which his reason would lead him, and this would be absurd.

Said the Rabbi: The divine Law does not impose asceticism upon us. It rather desires that we should keep to the golden mean, and allot to every mental and physical faculty its just share, without giving too much to one faculty and too little to another. One who inclines toward the faculty of lust, decreases his thinking faculty; and, on the contrary, he who inclines toward continence decreases some other faculty. Prolonged fasting is no act of piety for a man whose appetites are weak, whose faculties are feeble, and

---

[4] *Ibid.*
[5] Jeremiah 7. 21.

whose body is emaciated; he rather should pamper his body. Nor is the decreasing of wealth an act of piety, if it happens to have been gained in a lawful way, without trouble, and the acquisition thereof does not disturb him from occupying himself with knowledge and good deeds, especially for one who has dependants and children, and whose desire is to spend money for the sake of God; he rather should amass wealth. As a general rule, our Torah is divided into fear, love, and joy, by each of which one may draw near to God. Thy contrition on fast-days is not nearer to God than thy rejoicing on Sabbaths and festivals, provided thy rejoicing is with devout intention and perfect heart. Just as supplications require concentration of mind and devout intention, so also the rejoicing in His commandment and His Torah requires concentration of mind and devout intention; thou shouldst rejoice in the commandment itself, because thou lovest Him who enjoined it, and shouldst thereby acknowledge the bounty He bestowed upon thee. For thou art, as it were, enjoying His hospitality, being invited to His table and bounty, and shouldst thank Him for it inwardly and outwardly. Now if this rejoicing leads thee to singing and dancing, thou thereby worshippest God and cleavest unto the divine influence. These matters were not left by the Torah free to the discretion of man, but all were strictly regulated, since it is beyond the power of human beings to apportion to each faculty of the soul and the body its right measure, or to decide what amount of rest and movement is good for it, or to determine the quantity that the ground should produce, so that it may rest in the years of release and jubilee, and that tithes may be given thereof, and so forth. God commanded to rest on the Sabbath, to rest during the festivals, and that the earth should rest; all this as a remembrance of the going forth from Egypt, and as a memorial of the work of creation. These two things resemble one another, both having been accomplished by the will of God, not by accident or natural development; as He, who is blessed, says: 'For ask now of the days past, which were before thee.'⁶ 'Did ever a people hear the voice of God.'⁷ 'Or hath God assayed.'⁸ The observance of the Sabbath in itself has thus become an acknowledgment of the Godhead; nay, as it were, it is an acknowledgment of the creative utterance. For he who accepts the ordinance of the Sabbath, because the work of creation was finished on it, acknowledges the creation itself without doubt; and he who acknowledges the creation, acknowledges the Creator, the Maker, who is blessed. He, however, who does not accept it falls into the heresies of the world's eternity, and his belief in the world's Creator is not pure. Accordingly, the observance of the Sabbath brings one nearer to the Creator than do asceticism and monastic retirement. See how the divine influence, which had cleaved to Abraham and then to His chosen multitude, and to the Holy Land, kept on leading them from degree to degree, and guarded their posterity, so that none was detached. It put them in the best place, made them fruitful, and multiplied them in a miraculous manner, until it removed them, and planted them in a land worthy of a chosen people. He is therefore called the God of Abraham and the God of Isaac, just as He is called

⁶ Deuteronomy 4 32.
⁷ *Ibid*. 4. 33.
⁸ *Ibid*. 4. 34.

Dweller above the Cherubim, Dweller in Zion, and
Dweller in Jerusalem, these places being likened to
heaven, as it is written: ' O Thou that dwellest in
the heaven ', [9] for His light shines in these places, as
it shines in heaven, though only through mediums
worthy of receiving that light which He sheds upon
them.   This is called His *love,* which was established
for us, in which we are obliged to believe, and for
which we have to thank Him in the prayer *With
everlasting love dost Thou love us;* so that we should
bear in mind that it originated with Him, not with us.
To give an instance, we say concerning the creation
of a living being that it did not create itself, but God
formed and fashioned it, when He selected the matter
fit for that form.   In the same manner it was He,
who is blessed, who initiated our delivery from Egypt,
that we should be His own people, and He should
be our King, as He repeatedly says: ' I am the Lord
your God, who brought you out of the land of Egypt,
to be your God.' [10]   He also says: ' Israel, in whom I
will be glorified.' [11]

[9] Psalm 123. 1.
[10] See Leviticus 22. 33; the verse is modified.
[11] Isaiah 49. 3.

XXIV. MOSES B. MAIMON

[This great philosopher and Halakist, who is usually called Maimonides, was born at Cordova in 1135, and died at Cairo in 1204. He was endowed with a very clear and systematic mind, and exercised the greatest influence as philosopher and authority on the Talmud and Jewish jurisprudence. He was a very prolific writer, but his most important works are his *Guide of the Perplexed,* which was written in Arabic, his *Code,* written in Hebrew and known as the *Yad ha-Hazakah* (Mighty Hand), or *Mishneh Torah* (Repetition of the Law), and his Arabic commentary on the Mishnah. He was a physician by profession, and wrote several essays on medicine and astronomy.]

A Man Should Choose the Golden Mean [1]

Men have various dispositions, which are different from, and diametrically opposed to, one another. There is one man who is irascible, and is continually angry; while there is another who is of a calm disposition and does not get angry at all; and even if he gets angry, his wrath is mild, and this only happens once in several years. There is one man who is exceedingly haughty, while there is another who is exceedingly meek. There is one man who is voluptuous, whose soul can never be satisfied with indulging in pleasures; while there is another whose heart is so pure, that he desires not even the bare necessities which the body requires. There is one man who is exceedingly avaricious, whose soul cannot be satisfied with all the riches of the world, as it is written: 'He that loveth silver shall not be satisfied with silver;'[2] while there is another who is so unambitious, that he

[1] *Code, Hilkot De'ot,* chapter 1.
[2] Ecclesiastes 5. 9.

is content with a small thing which is hardly sufficient for him, and does not strive to obtain all that he needs. There is one man who emaciates himself by starvation, and saves all his money, and is very grieved when he has to spend a Perutah for his food; while there is another who wilfully squanders all his possessions. And in the same manner are all other dispositions, as for instance, one man is hilarious, while another is melancholy; one is niggardly, while another is generous; one is cruel, while another is merciful; one is faint-hearted, while another is courageous, and so forth.

Between two contrary dispositions which are at the two extremes there are intermediate dispositions which are likewise different from one another. There are some dispositions which are inherent in a man from his very birth, in accordance with the nature of his body; while there are others to which a man's nature is so predisposed, that they are readily adopted by him sooner than any other; and there are still others which are not inherent in a man from his very birth, but are acquired by him through imitating other men, or are adopted by him of his own accord because of an idea that occurred to him, or because, having heard that this disposition was good for him and worthy of being cultivated, he regulated his conduct accordingly, until it has become fixed in his heart.

The two diametrically opposed extremes of all dispositions are not the good way, and it behooves no man to walk therein, nor to adopt them. If a man finds that his nature inclines toward one of them, or is predisposed to adopt it, or that he has already acquired it, and regulated his conduct accordingly, he should return to that which is good, and walk in the way of the good ones, which is the right way.

The right way is the intermediate quality of every disposition of man, and that is the disposition which is equidistant from both extremes, being neither nearer to the one nor to the other. The ancient sages have therefore commanded that a man should always put, arrange, and direct his dispositions in the middle course, so that he may be sound in his body. In what manner? He should not be irascible, easily provoked to anger, nor as a dead man that is insensible, but should take the middle course: he should only get angry on account of an important matter, when it behooves to show anger in order that a similar offence should not be again committed. Similarly, a man should only desire those things which are necessary and indispensable for his body, as it is written: ' The righteous eateth to the satisfying of his desire.' [3] In like manner, he should not exert himself in his business more than to obtain the necessities of life, as it is written: ' A little is good for the righteous.' [4] He should not be too niggardly, nor squander his money, but should give charity according to his means, and in a fitting manner lend to him who is in need. He should not be hilarious and mirthful, nor gloomy and melancholy, but always happy and contented and of cheerful countenance. In the same manner should all his dispositions be. This way is the way of the wise; every man whose dispositions are intermediate, that is to say, in the middle course, is called wise.

A man who is very strict with himself, and removes himself from the middle course slightly toward one

[3] Proverbs 13. 25.
[4] Psalm 37. 16.

10

side or another, is called pious.   In what manner?
He who removes himself from haughtiness toward
the other extreme, and is very humble, is called pious;
and this is the quality of piety.   If, however, he moves
only as far as the middle, and is modest, he is called
wise; and this is the quality of wisdom.   In the same
manner are all other dispositions.   The pious men of
ancient times used to turn their dispositions from the
middle course toward the extremes; some dispositions were made to incline toward the one extreme,
while others toward the other extreme; this is beyond
the line required by the law.   We, however, are commanded to walk in middle courses, which are the
good and upright ways, as it is written: ' And thou
shalt walk in His ways.' [5]   In interpreting this commandment, the sages say: ' As He is called gracious,
so shalt thou be gracious; as He is called merciful,
so shalt thou be merciful; as He is called holy, so shalt
thou be holy.' [6]   And for this reason did the prophets
call God by all these attributes: slow to anger, abundant in lovingkindness, righteous, upright, perfect,
mighty, strong, and so forth, in order to let us know
that these are good and upright ways, according to
which a man is obliged to regulate his conduct, so
that he may be like unto Him, as far as lies in his
power.

In what manner should a man accustom himself to
these dispositions, so that they should become part of
his nature?   He should do once, and twice, and three
times the deeds which he is to do according to the
intermediate dispositions, and should always keep on
repeating them until they have become so easy for

[5] Deuteronomy 28. 9.
[6] Shabbat 133b; Sotah 14a.

him that he can do them without the slightest effort;
the dispositions will then become fixed in his soul.
Because the Creator is called by these names, they
are according to the middle course wherein we are
obliged to walk, and this way is called the way of God:
it is the one which Abraham taught his children, as
it is written: 'For I have known him, to the end
that he may command. . . . .'[7] And he who walks in
this way brings welfare and blessing to himself, as
it is written: 'To the end that the Lord may bring
upon Abraham that which He hath spoken of Him.'[8]

[7] Genesis 18. 19.
[8] *Ibid.*

XXV. JOSEPH B. MEIR IBN ZABARA

[Poet and physician. He was born in the city of Barcelona about the middle of the twelfth century. As a writer he is best known by his *Sefer Sha'ashu'im* (Book of Delight) which is a store-house of folk-lore and science. In this book, which is written in rhymed prose, Ibn Zabara shows himself abreast of the sciences of his day. His style is fluent and pleasant. He is also the author of liturgic and secular poems.]

Jacob the Broker and the Necklace [1]

There was a Jew in Cordova whose name was Jacob the broker. That man was good and faithful, readily obedient to the command of the judge. One day a necklace of choicest stones and pearls was committed to his care that he should sell it for five hundred pieces of gold. And it came to pass that, while he was carrying the necklace in his hand, a lord, one of the king's nobles, met him, and said to him: ' Jacob, what kind of a necklace is this?' He replied: 'My lord, it was handed over to me that I should sell it.'

' For how much wouldst thou sell it?'

He replied: 'For five hundred pieces of gold.'

The nobleman said to him: 'Wilt thou give it to me for four hundred?'

He replied: 'I cannot, for its owner warned me not to take for it less than five hundred pieces of gold.'

Whereupon the nobleman said: 'Take it to my house, and if it is good in the sight of the mistress of the house, I will buy it.'

So he walked with him until he reached the gate of his house. The nobleman then said: 'Stand here,

[1] *Sefer Sha'ashu'im*, Davidson's edition, pp. 49, *seq.*

148

until I have brought out unto thee the money or the necklace.' He entered the house, and closed the door behind him. The Jew waited until evening, but nobody came forth from the door of the nobleman's house.

And it came to pass at the going down of the sun that Jacob went to his house full of grief, so that death would have been pleasant unto his soul; care settled in his heart, and wounded it. He came home, and passed the night lying on the ground. He ate no bread, neither he nor his wife and children, and put not off his garments. He closed not his eyes and eyelids, and turned about as clay under the seal. He rose early in the morning to go to the house of the lord, and behold, he was coming forth from his house. When Jacob saw him, he ran to meet him, and said unto him: ' My lord, dost thou desire to buy the necklace, or wilt thou return it unto me that I may sell it to another man?' But he said: ' Which necklace? Hast thou seen one of the children of Anak?'' And Jacob said unto him: ' The pearl necklace which thou tookest yesterday from my hand.' Whereupon the nobleman said unto him: ' Madman, lunatic, as my soul liveth, and as the king's soul liveth, were it not that I regard my honor, I would have lifted up thy head from off thee, and would have covered thee with the blood of thy liver.'

And it came to pass, when Jacob saw his anger and the roughness of his words, that terrors of death fell upon him. He turned back, and fled from before him, for he saw that he sharpened his eyes upon him. He went to the house of the judge his master. The judge looked at him, and behold, grief bit him with its

[2] There is a pun in the original: *Anak* is a necklace as well as a name of a tribe of giants.

teeth, so that it changed his likeness and the appearance of his countenance. And the judge said unto him: 'What ails thee that thou art so changed? Art thou afflicted in aught?' He replied unto him: 'My lord, I am in great distress; but I cannot tell my trouble unto thee, lest thou shouldst declare me a liar, and make my speech nothing worth.' And the judge said unto him: 'Tell it to me, for in my sight thou art trustworthy in all thy words, and righteous in whatsoever thou sayest.' Whereupon he related to him all that had happened to him about the necklace, so that his soul chose strangling. The judge then said unto him: 'Put away vexation from thy heart, and remove grief from thee; be not in pain, and cry not in thy pangs, for I shall restore the necklace unto thee.'

And it came to pass in the morning that the judge sent for the nobles, elders, sages, and wise men of the city to come to the court; for it was his custom to send sometimes for the wise men, and to discuss points of law with them. And they all came to his house to hear the words of his understanding and his wisdom. Now before they came, he said unto his servant: 'When that nobleman comes, take his shoe,[3] and go to his house, and say unto his wife: " My lord thy husband sent me to thee that thou shouldst give him the necklace which he bought yesterday or the day before yesterday; for he desires to show its goodness and beauty; behold, he gave me his shoe for a testimony and for a sign." ' When the woman saw her husband's shoe, she gave him the necklace. The servant brought it to his master, and hid it in his bosom until the men went out from the house of judg-

[3] It is an Oriental custom to take off the shoes.

ment. And it came to pass, when they went out, that
his master said unto him: 'Hast thou brought the
necklace?' And he replied: 'I have brought it;'
and he took it out from his bosom, and gave it to him.
Then he sent and called Jacob the broker, and said
unto him: 'Be still, and groan not, for I have restored
the necklace unto thee, and have taken out from the
house of the nobleman the thing he gained by oppression.' When the Jew saw it, he kissed his hands and
blessed him. He carried it to his house, joyful and
glad of heart.

XXVI. SAMUEL B. JUDAH IBN TIBBON

[Physician and translator. He was born at Lunel about 1150, and died at Marseilles 1230. He continued the work of his father, and earned for himself the gratitude of Hebrew readers by translating Maimonides' *Guide of the Perplexed* into Hebrew. He also compiled a glossary of the philosophic terms that occur in that book. He was an enthusiastic follower of Maimonides.]

On the Limitations of Man's Intellect [1]

Know that there are objects of perception which are within the capacity and nature of the human intellect to grasp. There are in existence other things and objects which are not in its nature to perceive in any shape or form; indeed the gates of perception are closed against it. There are in existence still other things of which the intellect may grasp one part, while remaining ignorant of the other. Because the intellect has the power of grasping, it does not necessarily follow that it can grasp everything, just as there are objects of perception which the senses can perceive only at a certain distance, and no other. The same is the case with all other corporeal faculties. Thus, for instance, although a man is able to carry two kikkars, he is not able to carry ten. That individuals of the same species surpass one another in these sensations and other corporeal faculties is clearly manifest to every man; but there is a limit to individual superiority, which does not extend to every distance and degree. The same is the case with the perceptions of the human intellect. The individuals of the human

---

[1] Maimonides' *Guide of the Perplexed,* vol. I., chapter 31.

species greatly surpass one another in this respect. This, too, is clearly manifest to the men of wisdom. For while one man can discover a certain thing by himself through his own speculations, another man is never able to understand it; even if he is taught by means of all possible expressions and examples, and during a long period, his intellect can in no way grasp it, the power of his mind being insufficient to understand it. This distinction is likewise not unlimited. Indeed, the human intellect undoubtedly has a boundary where it must stop. There are certain things which are manifestly inaccessible to the understanding of man, so that his soul does not even long to know them, being aware of the impossibility of such knowledge, as there is no opening through which he may enter to attain to it. For instance, we are ignorant as to the number of the stars of heaven, whether it is even or odd; nor do we know the number of the species of animals, minerals, plants, and similar things. There are, however, other things to comprehend which man entertains a strong desire, and mental efforts to seek and investigate the truth thereof are made by every thinking sect of men at all times. It is with regard to these things that opinions differ, and thinkers disagree, and confusions constantly arise, because the intellect is bent on comprehending them, that is to say, on account of the longing entertained for them: every one thinks that he has discovered a way by which he may know the truth of the thing, whereas it is not within the power of the human intellect to produce demonstrative proof on the matter. (For every proposition, the truth of which can be ascertained by proof, is not subject to dispute, contradiction, or rejection; none but the

ignorant would join in a controversy which is known
as the ' controversy capable of demonstrative proof.'
Thus one finds that men disputed concerning the
spherical form of the earth, or the circular revolution of
the sphere, and the like. Such matters do not belong to
this treatise). Now as to the subjects in which this
confusion prevails, it is exceedingly frequent in metaphysical speculations, less so in matters relating to
physics, and is entirely absent from the exact sciences.
AlexanderAphrodisius says that there are three causes
which bring about disputes on various subjects :
firstly, love of authority and conquest which prevents
a man from attaining to the exact truth ; secondly, the
subtlety, depth, and difficulty of the subject which is
to be comprehended ; thirdly, the ignorance of
the investigator and the insufficiency of the power
of his intellect to comprehend that which may be comprehended. That is what Alexander states. In our
times there is a fourth cause which Alexander did not
mention, because it did not exist at that time, namely,
habit and training. For men naturally love and are
attracted by that to which they have been accustomed.
We thus see that villagers, although they seldom wash
their heads and their bodies, and, missing all pleasures,
lead a life of privation, nevertheless dislike the cities,
and do not enjoy their pleasures ; they prefer bad
things to which they are accustomed to good things
to which they are not accustomed. They derive no satisfaction from dwelling in palaces, from
being clad in silk, and from indulging in baths, oint-
ments, and perfumes. The same happens to a man
with reference to his opinions to which he has been
accustomed, and in which he has been brought up :
he cherishes them, defends them, and shuns the op-

posite views. It is likewise through this cause that a man is prevented from attaining to truth, and clings to the things to which he has been accustomed. Such, for instance, is the case with the vulgar notions concerning God's corporeality, and many other metaphysical questions, as we shall explain. This is due to long familiarity with scriptural verses, which, as a fixed dogma, were respected and believed in, and the literal sense of which implies corporeality of God and imageries in which there is no truth; these passages, however, were written as parables and allegories, for reasons which I shall mention below.

Do not think that that which we have said of the insufficiency of the power of the human intellect and of the limit where it must stop is an assertion made only in accordance with the Torah; in truth it is a matter which the philosophers have likewise asserted, and which they have comprehended in a true manner, without inclining to any doctrine or opinion. It is an established fact that can only be doubted by one who is ignorant of things that have been proved.

XXVII. JUDAH B. SOLOMON AL-HARIZI

[Celebrated poet of the twelfth and thirteenth centuries. Born in Spain, he travelled to the Holy Land and Babylon. He possessed a very vivid imagination and descriptive pen, and in his master-piece *Tahkemoni* he embodied the result of his experience during his travels. In that book, which is modelled after the *Makamat* of the famous Arabic poet al-Hariri, he shows himself a keen critic of men and things. He displayed marvellous skill in translating al-Hariri's book under the title *Mahberot Ithiel*. His style is fluent and melodious. He also translated Maimonides' *Guide of the Perplexed* into Hebrew, but in this work was less successful than Ibn Tibbon.]

Seven Young Men Discuss the Merits of the Various Virtues [1]

Heman the Ezrahite [2] saith: I was in the land of Pethor, the city of Balaam the son of Beor; and while I was walking by the riverside, under the shadows of plants and thickets of flowers, I perceived seven pleasant youths of the choicest society. They sat upon the bank of the river, making their hearts merry with words of rhetoric. One of them called out, and said: 'Which is the best quality that is more beloved than all other qualities and is the worthiest in the sight of God and man?'

One of them said: I know that all qualities are praiseworthy, but there is none as sublime as humility; for it conceals all faults, and reveals all that is beautiful; it causes to forgive transgressions, and makes its

[1] The nineteenth Makamah, or chapter of the *Tahkemoni*.
[2] This name of the biblical sage (comp. 1 Kings 5. 11) has been adopted for the name of the "narrator" (Al-Harizi himself?) who records the exploits and wonderful utterances of the "hero," Heber the Kenite.

possessor associate with the modest; it increases his
lovers and friends, and causes him to inherit a precious
and pleasant name. And he took up his parable, and
said: Amongst man's good traits there is none like
meekness: it is graceful and sublime to all the wise; it
stirs up love in hearts of enemies, and covers a man's
sins and transgressions.

His companion said unto him: From the right path
hast thou gone astray, and hast fed the wind. Humility or impudence is esteemed as nought when compared with promptitude; for with it a man conquers
souls, and finds favor and good understanding in the
sight of God and men, and inherits much honor and
greatness in this world and in the next; with it he
amasses increasing riches and houses full of all good
things. And he took up his parable, and said: It is
true that promptitude has no equal, and happy is he
who walks in its way; all precious qualities are but
handmaids, and promptness is like a queen to them.

His third companion said: Thou has spoken fool-
ishly, for there is no quality as good and precious
as courage and bravery; for with it a man subdues
all his enemies, and does good to his friends; he joins
himself unto the great, and will cry, yea, he will shout,
he will prove himself mighty against his enemies. He
will ascend the throne of excellence, so that they will
proclaim before him: ' Cast up the highway!' And he
took up his parable, and said: In truth there is no
precious trait in man like courage blended with
strength; indeed with it a man subdues his foes, and
brings them down with sorrow to the grave.

The fourth one said: Thou hast wandered out of
the way, and hast been made to serve folly with rigor;
for among all the qualities there is no quality as

worthy as faithfulness; for with it a man lifts up his
head, his soul becomes precious, and he is honored
in the sight of all flesh and blood, and finds favor and
good understanding in the sight of God and man
And he took up his parable, and said: Know there is
no quality as worthy in God's sight as faithfulness; if
prophecy assumed a mortal garb, it would appear like
faithfulness in form.

The fifth one said: There is no steadfastness in thy
mouth, and thy speech is without understanding; for
the most sublime quality is wisdom: it lifts up those
of its adherents that are low, and raises its banners
upon their heads; and wisdom preserves the life of
him that has it; if not for wisdom, man would not
excel an animal.   And he took up his parable and
said: In this our world there is no trait so sublime
and glorious to man's head as wisdom; with it a man
ascends the royal throne, and with it the weary ones
will find strength.

The sixth one said: A vain vision hast thou seen,
and falsely hast thou testified; for there is no quality
as good to any flesh as culture; for it is for his culture that a man is honored by those that know him,
and loved by those that hear him; they cover all his
transgressions; his memorial is pleasant to all mouths,
and his praise is like a tower built for an armory;
such a man is a delight to the heart, and his praises
endure for ever and ever.   And he took up his parable,
and said: There is no quality in man like culture; it
is majesty and grace unto all flesh; for if a man possesses all charms, but has no culture, know that he
lacks honor.

The seventh one said: Thou trustest in vanity, and,
following the east wind, feedest on wind; for

among all the qualities there is none as worthy as a
good heart; for through it a man is beloved of all
creatures, and is placed at the head of all guests; he
is honored in the sight of those that hear him and see
him, all that look upon him love him, and even his
enemies praise him; men laud him, and the angels of
heaven remember him for good. And he took up his
parable, and said: In truth there is no quality like a
good heart; with it a man will flourish like a watered
garden; through it he will be beloved of his Maker,
and will find favor and good repute in His sight.

When the old man heard their words, he said unto
them: Ye are all perplexed, and walk in darkness;
the right thing is hidden from you, and ye know not
to choose the truth; for among all the qualities there
is no quality as good as generosity; for all other qualities bow down at its feet, and it excels them all;
through it all sins are forgiven, and hatred is removed
from the heart; with it a man attains desirable things
that are far away, even if they are in heaven; through
it he is counted among the pious, for with it he does
righteous and kind deeds; with it he acquires a good
name, and his memorial is like precious oil. But he
who lacks generosity, his righteousness is counted as
guilt, his kindnesses as errors, and his favors as sins.
All his companions despise him, those who know him
hate him, his friends remember him for evil, and they
that dwell in his house and his maids count him for
a stranger. The bounteous man, however, lifts up
his countenance, for generosity covers all his sins, and
blots out his transgressions; his adversaries love him,
and his enemies praise him; they that are jealous of
him laud him, and they who would curse him bless
him. For by his generosity he conquers their hearts,

and attracts their love; through it haughtiness becomes beautiful, and faults turn into merits; through
it the fool is counted as wise, and the despised one
soars up to the heavens. Thus I have seen wicked
men who commit evil deeds, but if they have a generous heart, it conceals all their wickedness and guilt;
their bad qualities become good, and love covers
all transgressions. I have likewise seen men of faithfulness, prudence, and understanding, possessing all
worthy qualities; but if generosity is not among them,
fear of God becomes a sin, and humility haughtiness,
promptitude impudence, prudence folly, merit a fault,
and understanding lack of knowledge. For all other
good qualities bow down at the feet of generosity, and
concerning it it is written: ' Many daughters have
done valiantly, but thou excellest them all.' [3] And he
took up his parable, and said: It is true there are
precious traits in this world, but highest of all is generosity; for other traits, though they be praiseworthy,
stole their excellence from generosity.

The narrator said: When I heard his discourse and
the pleasantness of his instruction, I desired to investigate whether his wisdom is in accordance with his
rhetoric, and I said unto him: ' By the life of Him
who endowed thee with eloquent speech and a spirit
of counsel and might, make known to me the branch
of thy planting and the habitation where thou liest
down.'

And he answered, and said: I am Heber who compose a pleasant song, and flash forth flames of fire
from my tongue. I strengthen hearts with witty says-
ings which are set with stones of eloquence and meta-

[3] Proverbs 31. 29.

phors; I cover my friends with a cloak of praise, but clothe my foes with garments of dread.

When I heard his songs and his powerful words, I knew that he was our teacher and master Heber the Kenite our scholar. I stayed for a while with him to enjoy his fragrance and to satiate myself with the sweetness of his speech. Afterwards I greeted him with peace, and each man of us turned to his tent.

XXVIII. JUDAH B. SAMUEL HE-HASID OF REGENSBURG

[Ethical writer and mystic of the twelfth and thirteenth centuries. He died about 1217. Legend credits him with the performance of miracles. He founded a talmudic school, and among his pupils were Eleazar of Worms, author of the *Rokeah*, and Isaac of Vienna, author of the *Or Zarua'*. He is said to have had social intercourse with the bishop of Salzburg and the duke of Regensburg. His principal work is the *Sefer Hasidim* (Book of the Pious). He is also the author of some liturgic poems.]

Certain Forms of Virtue Lead to Sin [1]

There is a kind of humility which inherits Gehenna, and causes the heirs of the humble to inherit a burning fire in Gehenna. In what maner is it? If a man sees that his children, relatives, or pupils are of bad behavior, and it lies within his power to correct them, by reprimanding or by beating them, but he says to himself: ' I shall rather be agreeable to them and not reprimand or beat them,' he causes them to inherit Gehenna. For they will corrupt their way, and will even do mischief to their father and their mother, so that they will despise them, and curse the day wherein they were born. It is in connection with such a case that it is written: ' He that spareth the rod hateth his son.' [2] It is also said that he who smites his grown-up son transgresses the injunction: ' Put not a stumbling-block before the blind.' [3] But a son that is accustomed to reproofs of instruction, and is beaten while small,

---

[1] *Sefer Hasidim,* Judah Wistinetzki's edition, §§ 19024-19030.
[2] Proverbs 13. 24.
[3] Leviticus 19. 14.

will not resent if his father beats him when he is grown up. It is also written: 'Unless I had believed to see the goodness of the Lord;'[4] there are some dots on the word *Unless,*[5] for David said: 'Peradventure I caused my sons to sin, and am not able to make amends by repenting'; for it is written: 'And his father had not grieved him all his life in saying: "Why hast thou done so?"'[6]

There is another kind of humility which likewise brings a man down to Gehenna. For instance, a man sits in a court of justice, and knows that the judges are in error; or a private man knows that the court is in error, but says: 'How shall I go and put them to shame?' or a man knows that the judges are not well-versed in law, while he is well-versed, and when they say to him: 'Sit with us that we may not go astray', he replies: 'I shall not take a seat, for ye are well-versed.' It is obvious that if they go astray, the sin is to be attached to him. Another instance is, when a man hears that the congregation speak falsely, and he says: 'Who am I that I should speak before them?' Behold, it is written: 'And in thy majesty prosper, ride on, in behalf of truth and humility of righteousness'[7]; from this we infer that there is a kind of humility which is not righteousness, as the above and similar cases show. It is also said: 'An untutored priest should not say the benedictions in the presence of scholars.'

---

[4] Psalms 27. 13.
[5] The Rabbis usually give a homiletic reason for the dots that are placed over a word in the masoretic text of the Bible. See Berakot 4a.
[6] I Kings 1. 6.
[7] Psalm 45. 5.

There is a kind of charity which is pernicious.   In
what manner is it?   One who gives alms to adulterers
or to a glutton or a drunkard.   For it is written: ' She
shall not fall into harlotry,' [8] and thou mayest read:
' She shall not cause to fall into harlotry;' ' Thou
shalt not commit adultery,' [9] and thou mayest read:
' Thou shalt not cause to commit adultery.'   ' Thou
shalt not murder,' [10] and it may be read: ' Thou shalt
not cause to murder.'   He who supplies weapons of
destruction to murderers is regarded as if he himself
had committed murder.   For it is written: ' He hath
also prepared for him the weapons of death.' [11]   He
who gives food to robbers is like their accomplice.
Similarly, he who gives alms to adulterers is regarded
as though he had aided them and brought them together,
for they take the money that is given to them, and
offer it as a hire to harlots.   It is also said that a man
should give no alms at all rather than give it publicly. [12]   In a similar sense it is also said that if a man
who cannot pay his debts gives alms, it is obvious that
his charity is robbery.

There is a kind of piety which is bad.   For instance, a man whose hands are unclean sees a holy
book fall into the fire, and says: ' It is better that it
should be burned,' and does not touch the book.
Another instance has also been cited: a man sees a
woman drown in the river, and says: ' It is better
that she should drown than that I should touch her.' [13]

[8] Leviticus 19. 29.
[9] Exodus 20. 14.
[10] *Ibid*. 20. 13.
[11] Psalm 7. 14.
[12] Comp. Hagigah 5a.
[13] Sotah 21b.

There is also false piety. For instance: a man brings out a Scroll of the Law into the public thorough-fare on the Sabbath on account of a fire; or when a man says: 'How shall I save a man's life and profane the Sabbath?' Another instance is: a question about declaring a thing forbidden or lawful is referred to a man who knows that he is well-versed in the Law, though there are others like him in the city, and he says: 'Address the question to others;' behold, his meekness may lead to sin: peradventure if he had given his decision, he would have forbidden that which others had declared lawful.

There is sometimes a righteous judge that perishes in his righteousness. For instance: he sees two litigants, one being a swindler, and the other a simpleton; the swindler knows how to plead, but the simpleton, who does not know how to plead, is right; concerning him it is written: 'Open thy mouth for the dumb.'[14] Likewise, if he knows that the verdict is unjust, one of the litigants having hired false witnesses, he should not say: 'Let the sin be attached to the witnesses.'

A favor sometimes turns out to be harmful, and is regarded as an evil for its author and his offspring. In what manner is it? For instance: a man causes that sinners and they that lead others astray should dwell in the city. Now since it is bad for the people of the city, it is evident that he and his offspring will stumble over them, and they will do mischief to his offspring. It is in connection with such a case that it is written: 'And he did that which is not good among his people.'[15] (Another explanation: *And he*

[14] Proverbs 31. 8.
[15] Ezekiel 18. 18.

did that which is not good among his people refers
to him who disgraces his family; he is punished, because he sinned by inflicting shame and injury upon
his people). Another instance: he who does a good
deed in order to be honored and to praise himself
thereby.

XXIX. ELEAZAR B. JUDAH B. KALONYMOS OF WORMS

[Talmudist and mystic. He was born at Mayence about 1170, and died at Worms 1238. His teacher Judah he-Hasid initiated him in the mysteries of Kabbalah. His private life was cruelly tragic. In 1196, while he was engaged in writing a commentary on Genesis, the crusaders entered his house, and slew his wife and children. In spite of that, his writings are filled with spiritual joy, and he seems to soar above the calamities of the flesh. As a Halakist he was clear-sighted and logical, yet he was swayed by hallucinations, and saw angels and demons. He wrote numerous works on ethical, halakic, and mystical subjects. But the best known of his books is the *Sefer ha-Rokeah* (Book of the Perfumer). That book is so called, the author tells us, because the numerical value of the word רקח is identical with that of Eleazar.]

Moral Admonitions and Precepts [1]

O man that art born of a woman, consider the benefit and kindness thy Creator has bestowed upon thee since thou wast a wet, fetid, and white drop. See that thou art not ungrateful to Him. Thy father and mother forsook thee, but He took thee up, formed thee, and guarded thee, until thou camest forth from the womb. In the time of thy rejoicing know Him; thou shalt cause the fear of Him to come to thy mind, and all thy limbs shall tremble. Serve ye the Lord with joy, and rejoice with trembling: in the place of rejoicing, there shall be trembling; for by the sadness of the countenance the heart becomes glad. Think that the Creator is near thee: I have set the Lord always before me.[2] When thou

[1] Part of the Introduction to the *Sefer ha-Rokeah.*
[2] Psalm 16.8.

prayest, stand with awe, and think before whom
thou art standing, to whom thou art speaking. If
there is care in thy heart, dispel it during thy prayer;
for while standing before the Great King thou
shouldst not think of thy care, but of thy fear of Him
and of thy love of Him. For many there are who
sin against their souls: they sit in the synagogue like
mourners, their mouth being closed, and they sing not
to the Lord of hosts; they will be condemned to a fire
not kindled by man.

Therefore, for all these reasons, acknowledge Him
in all thy ways. Remove not the fear of the Lord
from thy heart. If thy sustenance is scanty, reflect:
'I ought to be satisfied with the breath which He
placed in my nostrils, and with the breath of my mouth.
He has given me poverty for my own good, to purify
me in the crucible of affliction!' If thy face grows
pale on account of thy fulfilling the commandments,
consider thy blood which was lost as the blood that is
sprinkled upon the altar. If thou art afflicted with
pain, accept it with love and with joy. Be wise in
thy fear of Him, for He is thy Master, and thou art
His servant owned by Him. Render thanks unto Him
for every measure. If He has given thee riches and
possessions, let thy heart not be lifted up above thy
poor brother, for thou knowest not what a day may
bring forth; ye both came forth naked from the womb,
and when thou departest from this world, thou like
him shalt lie down in the dust, in the place of worm
and maggots which shall go out and come in through
thy mouth. Even during thy lifetime thou mayest
be like him in need of the help of thy fellow-creatures.
If thou art punished through thy children, it should
be regarded in thy sight as though thou hast killed

them with thy sins. Murmur not against His measures, for the uproar of the tumultuous[3] is in them that occasion His judgment. Know that the Holy One is in thy midst; therefore conduct thyself with holiness, with saintliness, and with purity. When thou makest mention of the honored and awe-inspiring Name, let all thy limbs tremble. Set thy mind with devotion upon thy Creator, when thou standest in prayer. Before a word comes forth from thy mouth think of the interpretation of its meaning. If a worldly thought comes to thee in the middle of the prayer, keep silent until thou hast set thy mind upon the fear of the Creator. Be careful in uttering every word to move thy lips and to be conscious of the sound, in order that thou shouldst not commit an error; just as when counting money, thou settest thy mind and attention on the number. When thou standest up in prayer, say: 'I am not worthy of giving a crown to the King of glory and to mention His great name!' Clothe thyself with terror, as Abraham said: 'Behold now, I have taken upon me to speak unto the Lord, who am but dust and ashes.'[4] Say to thyself: 'Do not the sons of heaven fear and dread Him? for it is very tempestuous round about Him; how much more I, who am formed of clay, and have not the understanding of a man! I am despised in my life and despicable in my death. I shall rend the caul of my heart, and enter His gates with fear and humility.' For wherever we find His greatness there we also find His humility: I dwell in the high and holy place, with him also that is of a contrite and humble spirit.[5] There-

---

[3] Comp. Isaiah 9. 4.
[4] Genesis 18. 27.
[5] Comp. Megillah 31a. Isaiah 57. 15.

fore while thy spirit is yet in its sheath, think of the fear of thy Creator. Commit thy works unto the Lord, and thy purposes shall be established. The fear of the Lord is a fountain of life, that one may depart from the snares of death. Keep away from hastiness and perversion, from haughtiness and slothfulness. Cling firmly to humility and peace; be not envious of them that work unrighteousness, but of the fear of the Lord continually. And the stability of thy times shall be a hoard of salvation, wisdom, and knowledge, and the fear of the Lord which is His treasure. ' Can any hide himself in secret places that I shall not see him?' saith the Lord.[e] Are these not the eyes of the Lord which everywhere run to and fro? Know that beauty, strength, glory, jealousy, wisdom, riches, poverty, and the prevalence of the evil inclination are transitory. Know likewise that the observance of the commandments and the fear of the Lord extinguish the fire of the evil inclination. and that the Torah is a remedy to remove the evil thought.

[e] Jeremiah 23. 24.

XXX. MOSES B. NAHMAN

[Talmudist, mystic, and biblical exegete. He is usually called Nahmanides, and in Spanish Bonastruc de Portas. He was born at Gerona about 1195, and died in Palestine about 1270. Subsequent writers regarded him as a great authority on the Talmud and Halakah, and his reputation was perhaps second only to that of Maimonides. His biblical commentaries, too, have been very popular. He was compelled to have a public disputation with a convert to Christianity named Pablo Christiano, in 1263, at the court of Barcelona. He was a physician by profession.]

Ethical Letter, Praising Humility, Addressed to His Son [1]

Hear, my son, the instruction of thy father, and forsake not the law of thy mother. My son, my beloved, accustom thyself always to speak gently to every man, at all times and seasons : thereby thou shalt avoid anger which is a very bad and blameworthy disposition, for it leads to sin, as our teachers of blessed memory said: 'If one gets angry, it is regarded as if he worshipped idols.' [2] And all punishments of Gehenna have power over him, as it is written: 'Remove anger from thy heart, and put away evil from thy flesh.' [3] By the world *evil* Gehenna is meant, as it is written: 'Even the wicked for the day of evil.' [4] When thou avoidest anger, thou wilt bring to thy mind the quality of humility, and cleave unto it, for it is the best of all virtues, as it is written:

[1] *Iggeret ha-Ramban.*
[2] *Midrash Le-'Olam,* chapter 15 (Jellinek's *Bet ha-Midrash,* III., p. 117.
[3] Ecclesiastes 11. 10.
[4] Proverbs 16. 4.

'The reward of humility is the fear of the Lord.'[5]
The Mishnah likewise says: 'Be exceedingly humble
of spirit.'[6] Even our teacher Moses, peace be upon
him, was praised by this quality, as it is written:
'And the man Moses was very meek.'[7] It is also
through the merit of this virtue that the Torah was
given at his hand, and that he was called the teacher of
all prophets. He who attains unto this quality is beloved of Heaven, as it is written: 'With him also that
is of a contrite and humble spirit.'[8] When thou clingest
to the quality of humility, the quality of the fear of God
will come to thy mind; for thou wilt continually lay
to thy heart whence thou camest, and whither thou
art going (thou art worm and maggot in thy life
and in thy death), and before whom thou art destined
to render account and reckoning (before the supreme
King of kings, the Holy One, blessed be He, whose
glory fills the earth). It is also written: 'Do not I
fill heaven and earth? saith the Lord.'[9] It is also
written: 'Behold, heaven and the heaven of heavens
cannot contain Thee; how much less the hearts of
the children of men!'[10] When thou wilt consider all
this, thou wilt fear thy Creator, and guard thyself
against sin. By clinging to these qualities thou wilt
be in a state of perfection and sublimity, and wilt
continually be happy with thy lot; this latter, too, is
one of the good qualities, as the Mishnah says: 'Who
is rich? he who rejoices in his lot.'[11] If thy conduct
in according to the quality of humility and thou art

[5] *Ibid.* 22. 4.
[6] Pirke Abot 4. 4.
[7] Numbers 12. 3.
[8] Isaiah 57. 15.
[9] Jeremiah 23. 24.
[10] I Kings 8. 27 and Proverbs 15. 11.
[11] Pirke Abot 4. 1.

ashamed before every man, and thou fearest thy Creator, who gives thee life, so that thou sinnest not, the spirit of the Shekinah and the splendor of its glory will dwell upon thee, and thou wilt deserve the life of this world and of the world to come.

My son and my beloved, know assuredly that one who exalts himself above his fellow-men rebels against the kingdom of heaven, for he makes use of God's garment, as it is written: ' The Lord reigneth, He is clothed with pride.' [12] And God, who is blessed, says concerning the haughty man: ' I and he cannot dwell together in this world.' Accordingly, he who is haughty will be uprooted from the world.

Consider with thy understanding: Of what should a man be proud? of his wealth and honor? they surely belong to God, and He, who is blessed, bestows them upon man, as it is written: ' Both riches and honour come to Thee, and Thou rulest over all.' [13] It is also written: ' The Lord maketh poor, and maketh rich.' [14] Of his wisdom? Let him remember the explicit words of Scripture: ' He removeth the speech of men of trust, and taketh away the sense of the elders.' [15] It is thus evident that all comes from Him, blessed be He; in His anger He brings low the haughty, and in His favor He lifts up the lowly. Therefore, my son, make thyself humble, and remove thyself from haughtiness, so that the Lord may raise thee high.

Now, my son, I shall set forth for thee how thou shouldst conduct thyself according to the quality of humility, to follow it continually. Let all thy words be spoken with gentleness, with respect, with good

[12] Psalm 93. 1.
[13] I Chronicle 29. 12.
[14] I Samuel 2. 7.
[15] Job 12. 20.

manners, and with love; thy countenance should be
pleasant, and thy head bowed down. Thine eyes
should look downwards, and thy heart upwards. Do
not gaze too fixedly upon a man, when thou ad-
dressest him. Let every man be greater than thou
in thy sight. If he is rich, thou shalt honor him, as
did our saintly teacher who used to honor the rich.
If he is poor and thou art rich, thou shalt have mercy
and compassion on him, and honor the Lord with
thy substance. If thou art wiser than he, thou shouldst
consider that thou art guilty, and he is innocent; for
he sins unwittingly, while thou sinnest wilfully, as
the Rabbis of blessed memory said: ' The errors of
the sages are regarded as wilful sins.' [16] In all thy
thoughts, words, and deeds, at all times and seasons,
regard thyself as though thou stood before the supreme King of kings, the Holy One, blessed be He,
and as if His Shekinah were upon thee; for His glory
fills the whole earth. Thy words should be spoken
with terror and fear, with trembling and awe, as a
servant standing before his master. Take heed to
study the Law continually, day and night, for thereby
thou shalt be able to fulfil the commandments
thereof; it is thy life and the length of thy days.
When thou hast finished the reading of a book, thou
shouldst retain that which thou hast learned, in order to
fulfil that which is written in it, as far as thou art
able to fulfil. Thou shouldst continually search thy
deeds, every day, morning and evening, in order to
depart from evil and to do good. Thus all thy days
will be in perfect repentance.

During the prayer of the Eighteen Benedictions
thou shouldst remove all the affairs of this world from

[16] Baba Mezi'a 33b.

thy heart; think of no other matter except of fixing thy mind on the prayer with perfect devotion. Prepare and purify thy heart and mind before God, blessed be He; thereby thy prayer will be pure, clean, untainted, full of devotion, and acceptable before the Holy One, blessed be His name, as it is written: ' Thou wilt direct their heart, Thou wilt cause Thine ear to attend.' [17] Death and life are in the power of the tongue, and he that keeps his mouth and tongue, keeps his soul from troubles. Therefore in every matter think of thy words before thou givest utterance to them, all the days of thy life, so that thou mayest not sin; thereby thy thoughts, words, and deeds will be upright and good.

My son, read this epistle once a week with thy friend, and walk continually after God, blessed be He, in order that thou mayest prosper in all thy ways and be worthy of the world to come which is stored up for the righteous. Whenever thou readest it, thou wilt get an answer from Heaven to all petitions which thou mayest ask from this time forth and for evermore.

[17] Psalm 10. 17.

XXXI. SOLOMON B. ABRAHAM IBN ADRET

[Celebrated authority on Halakah and zealous defender of traditional Judaism. He was born at Barcelona in 1235, and died in 1310. He was exceedingly active as Rabbi and author. His numerous responsa have been recognized as an important source for the internal history of the Jews in the thirteenth century.]

Epistle Prohibiting Anyone Under Twenty-Five Years of Age to Study Philosophy [1]

What avails it to refrain oneself, and who can refrain himself from speaking? Who shall comfort us in the grief of our heart, even though Ithiel and Ucal[2] stood before us? Shall Calcol, and Darda, and Heman[2] be able to heal the proud waters and the afflicted of the time? Unto whom of the holy ones shall we turn, and who is the faithful of the generation to bring the balsam from Gilead for the tottering foot and for the wound of long continuance? It is in the place of judgment and in the place of righteousness that we have seen many cracks, but there is none to repair the breaches. O land, land, land, where the men of renown were born, in whose midst was the Law of God, and upon whose heart was the breastplate of judgment; there thrones for judgment had been set, attended by the holy seed, the judge and the litigant.

[1] This epistle, which is in rhymed prose, is the second of a series of three letters written on this subject. In vehement language the author denounces those who make light of the words of the Law, and prefer philosophy to the word of God. The three epistles were written with the consent of the Jewish community at Barcelona.

[2] Names of wise men mentioned in the Bible; comp. Proverbs 30. 1; I Kings 5. 11.

And even up till this day all the congregation, with
the exception of a few men, are holy; they are the
elect of the congregation, and because of their excellence are chiefs over all the people. But their
children who arise after them have created a waster
to destroy; and as a band of prophets, with harp and
lute, they go about the city, and pursue vanity. When
they spoke their fearful words, they thought that they
were exalted in Israel; and at the head of every street
they said concerning false gods: ' These are thy gods,
O Israel.' It is now some time since our attention
has been drawn by people from the land of Provence,
the chosen remnant, who were jealous for the faith
of Moses and the Jews, to the fact that there are men
there who falsify the Law, and that he is regarded
wise who sits down to demolish the walls and who
destroys the words of the Law. They hew out for
themselves cisterns, broken cisterns, and they impute
unto the words of the Law and the words of the
sages things which are not right. Concerning the
two Laws they expound in the synagogues and in
the houses of study words by which none can live.
To provoke the eyes of the Glory of all Israel they
break down all the fences of the Law; and even
against our holy fathers they put forth their tongue,
a thing which the worshippers of idols have not done.
For they say that Abraham and Sarah represent
matter and form, and that the twelve tribes of Israel
are the twelve constellations. Has a nation ever heard
such an evil thing since the world was divided into
territories? Or has such a thing ever been heard,
that men should reduce everything to chaos? The
blasphemers of God further say that the holy vessels
which were sanctified, the Urim and the Thummin, are

12

the instrument known as astrolabe, which men make for
themselves. Have such false children ever been found
before? They in truth bite the people more danger-
ously than do the fiery serpents. Without any benefit and without any cause they commit the sin of
slander, and say that the four who fought against
the five [3] are the four elements and the five senses.
May the souls of these men be wholly consumed as
offerings! A man who does such things reduces the
entire Bible to useless allegories; indeed they trifle
with, and pervert all the commandments in order to
make the yoke of their burden lighter unto themselves.
Their reports terrify us, and all who arrive here tell
us new things. Truth has stumbled in the street, for
some of them say that all that is written from the sec-
tion of *Bereshit* as far as the giving of the Law is nothing more than an allegory. May such men become a
proverb and a by-word, and may they have no stay
and no staff. Indeed they show that they have no
faith in the plain meaning of the commandments;
they inscribe on their hearts and on the walls of their
altars that they have no portion in the God of Israel,
nor in the Torah which their fathers had received on
Sinai. They are more estranged than the Gentiles;
for the latter fulfil some of the commandments in
the proper form, while they (may they have no remnant in the land!) strongly desire to uproot all. The
chief reason of all this is because they are infatuated
with alien sciences, Zidonian and Moabitish, and pay
homage to the Greek books. They mingle with strangers, and bear them children. The children that are
consecrated unto heaven from their birth and from
their mothers' womb are drawn away from the breasts,
and are taught the books and the language of the

[3] The allusion is to Genesis 14. 1-15.

Chaldeans, instead of rising early to study the Jewish faith in the house of their teachers. Now a boy born upon the knees of natural science, who sees Aristotle's sevenfold proofs concerning it, really believes in it, and denies the Chief Cause; if we refute him, he becomes all the more impious. They only read the Law, but their heart is not right inwardly, and they pervert it in seven ways. For thus says one of their sages, who is esteemed as the chief of the heads of their sects: ' It is good that the study of the Law should be combined with secular sciences; it is a good thing, but without the wisdom of the Greeks a man is called *a wild ass used to the wilderness.* They that study the Law, what manner of wisdom is in them? for they themselves are but as beasts.' They are therefore ashamed when they speak and lecture; they speak with their mouths, and point with the fingers that it is impossible to change nature, and they thereby declare to all that they do not believe in the creation of the universe, nor in any of the miracles that are recorded in the Torah. Lo, these are but the outskirts of their ways; were we to relate the rest of their words and deeds as they actually are, the ink would not suffice. We have thus explained enough here. They have nearly caused God's people to forget His name; they went forth from His land, so that His place (God forfend!) no longer knows them. They that make a covenant with God, and surname themselves by the name of Israel, shall not their heart grow hot at that? Can those heretics put fire into our bosoms, and their flame not consume our reins? Shall the lovers of the Law respect the person of their brother or kinsman? Has the divine word completely gone away? Has instruction failed? Shall it be said unto my children, as these men actually say in our presence: ' Let the Law return to Sinai '?

Now when we saw that the fire was kindled, we feared lest the fire should break out, and catch in thorns, namely, a man whose soul is empty, who will be smitten through ignorance. God forbid that the earth should become empty, and void, and waste! When we saw that the generation had become corrupted and ready to treat religion lightly, we made a fence, and strengthened the wall round our perfect Torah. Had we not made a strong hedge round the vineyard of the Lord of hosts, we would have shared in the blame for their deeds. We have therefore interdicted in a perfect manner of interdiction, as ye see recorded with writing of truth in the book of the covenant which we made with our God,[4] any one to teach or to learn these sciences, until the student and the teacher are twenty-five years old, and until they have become full of the delicacies of the Law, so that they will not remove it from being queen; for he who espouses it in his youth will not turn away from it even when he grows old. And indeed we shall not have done our duty, until we have pursued them, and brought them low, and removed the abominations from between their teeth; the books which they composed should be burned in the public place in their presence. It is about three years now since we have endeavored to carry out our wish in accordance with our aim; we have made many supplications, asking, requesting, and praying, to restore the crown of the Torah to its pristine glory, in its place. All this did we, so that the sword should not be against the dove which is foolish and without understanding, and that we should

---

[4] The allusion is to the first epistle.

not afterwards be reviled by the mouth of the reviler. Our words, however, did not enter into their ears; they made their words, which are directed against us, harsher still, because of their ability to write and to speak. Nevertheless we did not cease to write to them. But many strict communities of those provinces inscribed their name to God, and decided to ban and excommunicate them, and they acted wisely after us, as ye see from the copies of their letters.

Now, ye chiefs of righteousness, is the thing good in your sight? For the thing which they do is not good, and the report which the people of the Lord caused to transpire is not good. Far be it from us, lest the nation should be divided into two, and God forbid that the name of Heaven should be profaned through them. For it is really the duty of every Israelite to tell them that. We have trustworthy evidence in that which the Israelites did, when the children of Gad and the children of Reuben built an altar on the other side of the Jordan.[5] Did they not hasten to assemble for war on account of the suspicion of the intention? How much more have we to do it, since these men destroy the cluster [6] in the sight of all! Far be it from us that, by hiding our face from the evil report, we should be included in the prophet's accusation: ' There they stood; no battle was to overtake them in Gibeah.' [7]

Ye mountains of Israel, may ye bear your fruit for ever! ye people of the God of Abraham, set your eyes upon the palace,[8] lest their folly should destroy the fence of the Law. Let us be one band, for we are all the children of one man. With many covenants we

[5] The reference is to Joshua 22. 10-34.
[6] That is, traditional Judaism.
[7] Hosea 10. 9.

and our fathers received truthful Laws, written and oral, at the hands of the master of the prophets. How can we deal falsely against our soul and entice our heart to seek the deceptions of Greek philosophy? They vhose eyes go in front of them, how can they walk with their faces backward and ally themselves with Arabic philosophy? Arise, ye princes, anoint the shield, and the Lord shall defend you and your houses; for the Master of your work is faithful to pay the reward of your labor.

XXXII. JEDAIAH HA-BEDERSI

[Poet, philosopher, and physician. He was born in Béziers about 1270, and died about 1340. As a boy he was very precocious, and composed a prayer of a thousand words, each word beginning with the letter מ. Being an eloquent writer, he earned for himself the title *ha-Meliz* (the Rhetorician). He was the author of several treatises in prose and poetry, but his fame rests upon the *Behinat 'Olam* (Examination of the World).]

The Nothingness of Man and His Pursuits [1]

The world is a tempestuous sea of immense depth and breadth, and time is a frail bridge constructed over it, the beginning of which is fastened with the cords of chaos that preceded existence, while the end thereof is to behold eternal bliss, and to be enlightened with the light of the King's countenance. The width of the bridge is a cubit of a man, and it lacks borders. And thou, son of man, against thy will art thou living, and art continually travelling over it, since the day thou hast become a man. When thou considerest that the path is narrow and that there is no way to turn either to the right or to the left, shalt thou glory in position and fame? When thou seest that destruction and death are unto thee a wall on thy right and on thy left, shall thy heart endure, or shall thy hands be strong? Even if thou pridest thyself with the desirable acquisitions and the abundance of possessions which thou hast amassed and discovered with thine arm, hast sought with thy bow, and hast gone down to possess with thy net, what wilt thou do

[1] *Behinat 'Olam,* chapters 8 and 9. Soncino edition (1484).

against the tempest of the sea and the roaring thereof, when it rages, overflows, and passes through, so that even thy dwelling-place is about to be broken? Glory thou over this immense sea in whose midst thou art; rule over the horsemen and chariots thereof; go out now, I pray thee, to fight against it. For even while thou reelest to and fro and staggerest with the wine of thy rebellious arrogance which deceived thee, and with the juice of the pomegranates of thy haughtiness which misled thee, thou wilt soon incline slightly toward one side or another, and wilt perish in the terrible depths, and none will seek thy blood from them; thou wilt go from abyss to abyss, perplexed in the depths of the sea, and none shall say: ' Restore.'

Shall I trust in falsehood, shall I rely upon the staff of the bruised reed, to consider a lodging-place of wayfarers like this as a strong fortress and a king's sanctuary, the wing of a flea as a point of diamond, a spider's web as coral and crystal? When thou seest that the days are pleasant, that time frisks and dances, that the moment goes on to give thee repose, and that the hour frolics and rejoices before thee in the world, thou wilt despise the latter days in thy heart. But it is in falsehood that thou trustest: thou seest the shadow of a gourd as though it were a high and lofty mountain. Is it for these things that thou hast cast the soul behind thy back, and hast turned thy way toward the pleasures of the flesh which cause grief? Whenever thou seest that thy soul loves her God, being mindful of her end, and preparing provisions for her journey with the labor of her hands, thou enragest her; whenever she goes up to the house of the Lord, thou provokest her. Shalt thou forsake eternal glory and everlasting delight for the vanities of imaginary pleasures? And it shall come to pass, when thy heart will ask thee to-morrow, when the vicissitudes of time will leap upon thee: ' Who has begotten me these?' that thou shalt answer: ' The stubbornness of thy heart and its evil counsel.' If a servant spoils the work apportioned to him, will the spirit of the ruler not despise him? If a man walks about with his master without acknowledging him, will he not hate him?

Wilt thou pride thyself, O mighty man, when thou grazest in the green pastures after the youths in the presence of the sun, when thy stones are set in fair colors in midday, with the multitudes of thy companions? They say to themselves: ' Eat and drink ', but they have no heart. They only possess bodies and imaginary height of stature: vainglorious and corporeal things which have no spirit. Knowest thou not that there is a record of thy deeds, and that above thee there is an eye that sees and an ear that hears thine arrogance and raging? And now on whom trustest thou to break down the fences which the mightiest of the shepherds have founded? Is there no God above thee to know thy going out and thy coming in? Are no graves beneath thee wherein to take vengeance on God's enemies? How is it then that thou didst not lay it to thy heart that these vicissitudes which befall thee are the messengers of Providence? They turn not aside when they go to reward or to punish the individuals of mankind or the sects thereof. It is out of the mouth of the Most High that the decree comes to lay the noble low and to set the ignoble on high. When the base man goes up on the ladder of success, it has been brought about by the Lord; and when the man of God goes down from his high place, it is the King who has said: ' Go down.'

How is it that thou didst not open thine eyes upon these things? Have presumptuous thoughts and idle meditations deluded thee, and prevailed over thee? In the day the lustful reins have given thee counsel, and yet in the night seasons they have chastised thee with whips. With the venom of asps, mixed with the poison of serpents, did they make the clods of indolence sweet unto thy palate. With wanton words did they corrupt, make abominable, and mar for thee every good portion; salvation did they spoil with the flattery of words that are softer than oil. What meanest thou, O sleeper? How did they deceive thee by making thee forever the possessor of the riches of such lands, while thou art merely a sojourner for an appointed time in the innermost part of thy house? Cursed be they, for they have driven thee out that thou shouldst not cleave unto the inheritance of the holy ones, from whose rock thou wast hewn, and that thou shouldst not mingle in the assembly of the holy beings that gave thee life (but the lions' dens became thy dwelling-place). If, because of the hoards of gold and the treasure of provinces which thou didst amass, thou hast added haughtiness to thy pride, and hast humbled the generous spirit before it, see then how thou art beaten with the rod of folly and the plagues of blindness. Hast thou, because of the treasures of darkness which thou didst bind up, despised the soul that is bound in the bundle of life? Hast thou, for the sake of pieces of silver, crushed and suppressed a truthful longing and a glorious desire? Verily the glory of wealth lasts not. In a little while an evil spirit of the Lord shall come forth to scatter thy

possessions, and the fifty thousand pieces of gold, for
the sake of acquiring which thou has sold thy soul,
shall be as though they had not been. Time will turn
round in a little moment, and take away grace and
glory from thy head. A fire shall come down from
heaven, and consume thee and thy fifty.

Why shall I covet the earth which is like Admah
and pleasure which is like Zeboim? [2] Her wrath is
stored up in her company; her conspiracy is tightly
fastened to her covenant; her sweetness and honey-
comb are like chaff before the whirlwind; her end
and conclusion are eternal disgrace and everlasting
shame. Moreover, how can my flesh be delighted
when it is announced to me that I shall live long,
since there is no escape from the destruction of death?
What avails the age of strength, since at the end
thereof come wrath and the grave? What pleasure is
there in eighty years, since by their side is the shadow
of death? What cheerfulness is there in ninety years,
since there is no salvation in their border? Shall ants
that languish and perish, and creeping things that
melt away like water, exalt themselves to reign? Even
if they endure for a day or for two days, will they
never be devoured with the sword? How can the
fields of Sodom and the sheaves of Gomorrah prosper?

[2] Comp. Deuteronomy 29. 22.

XXXIII. IMMANUEL B. SOLOMON
OF ROME

[Italian scholar and satirical poet. He was born at Rome
about 1270, and died at Fermo in the first half of the fourteenth century. He excelled as poet, and his style is vivid and
fluent. His best known work is *Mahberot 'Immanuel,* which is
modelled after al-Harizi's *Tahkemoni.* He boasts, however,
that he surpassed his model, and in some respects this is not
without justification.]

The Poet Visits Paradise [1]

While we walked to and fro through the streets of
Eden, and looked upon the gallery of the men of wisdom, I perceived men full of splendor and majesty,
compared to whose beauty the sun and moon are
dark; a place was given them in the world of angels.
Not recognizing any one of them, I asked the man
who talked with me, that I might know concerning
them. And he said unto me: These are the pious
of the Gentiles, who prevailed with their wisdom and
intellect, and ascended the degrees of the ladder of
wisdom in accordance with their ability. They were
not as their fathers, a stubborn and rebellious generation; but they investigated with their intellect as to
who is the Maker, and who the Creator that fashioned
them with His lovingkindness, took them out from
nothingness to existence, and brought them to this
world; and as to what is the purpose for which He
created them. When they asked their fathers, and

[1] This is part of the twenty-eighth composition of the
Mahberot 'Immanuel, and is entitled *ha-Tofet we-ha-'Eden*
(Hell and Paradise). It is written in a manner similar to that
of Dante's *Divine Comedy.*

considered their answers, they knew that they were
worthless; they despised their creed, and set their
mind to investigate the creed of other nations. Having investigated all the creeds, and having found that
the hands of each of them are steadfast in strengthen-
ing its own foundations and in disparaging other
creeds, they did not say: ' Let us remain in our creed,
for it has been handed down to us by our fathers,'
but out of all creeds they chose those doctrines which
are true, and concerning which the wise men did not
differ; these doctrines they accepted, and to them they
clung. But to those opinions which all nations dis-
parage they turned their back, not their face. As regards God, they arrogantly call Him by a name at
which our heart trembles and shudders, for every
nation calls Him by a special name. We, however,
say: ' Let His name be what it may, we believe in
the truly First Existence, that produced life; that was,
is, and will be; that created the universe, when His
wisdom so decided; that is hidden from us through
the intensity of His revelation; that faints not, and
is not weary, and of whose understanding there is no
searching; that has mercy upon His creatures, and
feeds them, as a shepherd tends his flock; who will
call us unto Him, when our end draws nigh, and whose
glory will gather us together.'

When we ascended the steps of Eden, we saw
wonderful things, for there were set lofty and exalted thrones that appeared to my sight exceedingly
marvellous, so that the eye could not be satisfied with
seeing. Among them was one throne, the radiance of
which filled the world with splendor; it was like the
work of bright sapphire, and like the very heaven for
clearness. Its footstool had long edges, and the

bright metal thereof flashed continually; I longed
to sit upon it, and I said: 'I pray thee, my lord, for
whom is this honored and pleasant throne, and for
whom is the footstool of image work?' And he said
unto me: 'As thou livest, this throne is prepared for
the mightiest of the shepherds, and for him shall it
be; that is Judah, the lion's whelp, who prevailed
above his brethren. The footstool with its flowers
and buds is for the lawgiver that departeth not from
his presence. And thou shalt sit near him, and
shalt be close unto him.' And it came to pass, when
I heard these words, that I remembered the rank of
Daniel [2] my brother, who had led me in the right way,
and directed my path, and who had been near me when
I fled. He is the plate of the holy crown upon my
forehead, the life of my flesh and the breath of my
spirit. I thought of the full account of his greatness,
of his generosity and excellence, of his prudence and
understanding, of his humility and righteousness, and
of his renown which fills the ends of the earth. I
then said unto the man who held my right hand: 'I
pray thee, my lord, show me the place of Daniel and
his habitation; what manner of house do ye build for
him, and what place is his rest?' And he said unto
me: 'Know of a certainty that his rank is very high,
and that the ends of the earth are full of his renown;
even thy rank is too low to reach him. For he bore
the sin of many, and made intercession for the transgressors. But because the Highest Wisdom knew
that without thee he would find no rest and no repose,
it placed thy booth near his booth, though thy worth
is less than his; for the Highest Wisdom knew that
he will have delight in thy company: he would be

[2] This is supposed to be Dante his friend.

Moses, and thou wouldst be Joshua unto him ; in order
that all may declare, as it is said : Your souls are united,
they cling together, and cannot be sundered. Will
two walk together, except they have agreed ? '

There is nothing to marvel at that I was joyful, for
I knew that my lot fell in pleasant places, being aware
that I shall have redemption on account of him. And
I said unto the man : ' As thou livest, show me the
splendor of his throne, where he rests. For I know
that its height mounts up to the heavens, and its head
reaches unto the clouds.' And the man said unto me :
' Come with me, and I shall show thee his joy and
the glory of his resting-place.' So I went after him,
led and supported by him, until he brought me to the
tent of Oholiab the son of Ahisamach, where were
also Bezalel the son of Uri the son of Hur of the tribe
of Judah, and all the princes of the congregation.
Angels kept on bringing material for the work, and
were making pleasant and beautiful canopies that shone
like the brightness of the firmament, whose covering
was of every precious stone, and whose structure was
of sapphire, and tables, lamps, thrones, and crowns for
the pure souls. We saw there a big ivory throne overlaid with gold, which gave life to him that finds it,
and health to all his flesh. Crown stones glittered
upon it, and garments of blue and purple and scarlet
were spread over it ; they sparkled like burnished
brass, the glory of all lands. Upon the top of the
throne was a crown, the weight of which was a kikkar
of gold, and a precious stone that cannot be obtained
for fine gold, nor can silver be weighed for the price
thereof. A voice was saying : ' Proclaim that the
merchandise thereof shall be for them that dwell before the Lord.' And the man that talked with me said :

' Hast thou seen the crown and the lofty throne whereupon thy brother Daniel rises as a lion, and lifts himself
up as a lioness? This is his resting-place for ever,
and here shall he dwell, because he hearkened to the
word of the Lord, and there is no sage or thinker like
him in all the earth.' Thereupon I rendered praise
and thanks unto my Lord, because He brought him
to the rest and to the inheritance; and I said: ' Blessed
be the Lord who is one, and who has no second, because
He has not forsaken His lovingkindness and His truth
toward my master.'

When we ascended to the higher steps of Eden, we
saw a thing whereat we marvelled; for there we saw
men who during their life were ravenous beasts, bad
to God and bad to men; they died as wicked men the
death of them that are slain; their blood was poured
out as water, and their flesh as dung. When I saw
them shine like the brightness of the firmament, their
height mounting up to the heavens, and their head
reaching unto the clouds, I said in my heart: ' Behold,
the Lord has forgiven the sin of many, and makes
intercession for the transgressors.' I then inquired
of the man that talked with me, that I might know the
reason why these men deserved this lofty rank. And
he said unto me: ' These men sinned, dealt perversely,
and transgressed; for their sin they perished before
their time, and were filled with bitterness; they were
delivered into the hands of cruel people, and fell
wounded, having been pierced through, into the lions'
dens and upon the mountains of the leopards; they were
left together unto the fowl of heaven and unto the ravenous birds of the mountains. When they approached
the bitterness of death, they recalled the wickedness they
had done, and accepted the bitterness of death with love,

knowing that it came to them as a just retribution.
Death was more pleasant unto them than life, because
they considered that they deserved a greater calamity,
and that through these sufferings they were redeemed
from a severer punishment than death. When at the
point of dying they showed their joy and delight with
their mouth and heart ; and because they had received
part of their punishment in the corrupt world, wrath
was averted from their souls. Their death having
been cruel and bitter, it was accounted as a crown of
glory and a diadem of beauty upon the head of their
souls. It is, therefore, because of their death that they
deserved this glorious rank.'

XXXIV. JUDAH B. ASHER

[German Talmudist. He was born in Germany in 1270, and died in 1349 at Toledo where he was rabbi. He was a son of the great talmudic authority Asher b. Jehiel, known as the *Rosh,* and brother of Jacob, author of the famous code entitled *Turim.*]

Ethical and Moral Admonitions[1]

Take heed that ye belong not to the following four sects which will not see the Presence of God:

THE SECT OF LIARS. Let no false and deceitful matter be found in you, but truth and faithfulness shall be the girdle of your loins. There was a man in our family, named Rabbi Eliakum, who was in the house of the governor, and was entrusted with everything. The governor boasted to his own people that this Eliakum never uttered any falsehood, whether he derived any benefit, or not. It is narrated that there was once a wicked man who committed all kinds of sins. One day he asked a wise man to teach him the way of repentance in an easy manner, and the latter said to him: 'Refrain from telling lies.' He went forth joyful and glad of heart, thinking that the wise man permitted him to walk in the stubbornness of his heart as heretofore. When he determined to steal, as had been his custom, he reflected: 'What am I to do in case somebody asks me: "Whither art thou going?" If I tell the truth: "To steal," I shall be arrested; if I tell a lie, I shall transgress the command of the wise man.' In the same manner he reflected

[1] Part of the ethical will of Judah b. Asher. Schechter's edition, pp. 11, *seq.*

194

on all other sins, and repented with a perfect repentance.

THE SECT OF SCOFFERS. Be ye not scoffers, lest your bands be made strong,[2] and lest a fire consume your spirit. Guard yourselves against mockery and derision, for it is forbidden that a man should fill his mouth with laughter in this world. Be not merry on account of money, for this is likewise the way of robbers.

THE SECT OF FLATTERERS. Take heed that ye flatter not any man, and respect no person in judgment.

THE SECT OF THOSE THAT TALK SCANDAL. Be very much on your guard against this thing, for it leads to many sins; most men stumble over it. Our teachers of blessed memory said in tractate Baba Batra: ' Most men are prone to robbery, few of them to incest, and all of them to slander.'[3] The last part is explained as referring to something which resembles slander. Our teachers of blessed memory also said: ' Let no man talk of his friend's merits, if he may thereby be led to blame him.'[4] To all such cases refers the saying: ' I have not found for the body anything better than silence.'[5] A man should always think before speaking: if there is any profit in his speech, he should speak, otherwise he should be silent; how much more should he abstain from speaking, if there is harm in his speech!

Guard yourselves against pride, for every one that is proud is the abomination of the Lord. Pride is God's garment, and he who makes use of the crown shall perish. A wise man has said: ' How can a man be

[2] Comp. Isaiah 28. 22.
[3] Baba Batra 165a.
[4] 'Arakin 16a.
[5] Pirke Abot 1. 17.

proud, having passed twice through the womb?'
Cling to humility, for it is the best of all qualities, and
it is for this virtue that Moses our teacher, peace be
upon him, was praised, as it is written: 'And the man
Moses was very meek.'[6] And our teachers of blessed
memory said: 'Be exceeding humble of spirit.'[7]
Our teachers of blessed memory also said: 'That
which wisdom made a crown for its head did humility
make a sandal for its heel.'[8]

Take care to honor every man, that ye may thereby
be honored, as it is written: 'For them that honor Me
I will honor.'[9] Some people asked a wise man:
'How is it that we always see thee honor every man?'
He replied: 'I have not seen a man in whom I do not
discover an advantage over me for which I should
honor him. If he is old, I say: "This man performed
more good deeds than I." If he is rich, I say: "This
man gave more alms than I." If he is young, I say:
"I committed more sins than he." If he is poor, I say:
"This man suffered pain." If he is wiser than I, I
honor him for his wisdom. If he is not wiser than I,
I say: "His punishment is lighter than mine."' Hear
this, and know it for yourselves.

Be also careful to love and respect him who reproves
you. We thus read in the tractate 'Arakin, in the
chapter *There Are Estimations:* Rabbi Johanan says:
'I call heaven and earth to testify against me that
Akiba was beaten several times on account of me, because I used to complain against him to Rabban
Gamaliel; and yet he loved me all the more for that,

[6] Numbers 12. 3.
[7] Pirke Abot 4. 4.
[8] Yerushalmi Shabbat 3c, in commenting on Psalm 111. 10
and Proverbs 22. 4.
[9] I Samuel 2. 30.

in order to fulfil that which is written: " Reprove a wise man, and he will love thee.'' [10]   A wise man has said: ' Love him who reproves thee, and hate him who lauds thee ; for he who reproves thee benefits thee, while he who lauds thee harms thee.'

Consider also that man is a sojourner on earth, his days are counted and he knows not their number; nor does he know when he will be summoned before the King of kings to render account and reckoning of all that he has done. He should therefore perform all the good deeds he can ; and let no commandment be too small in his sight, for there is no limit to its reward. In the world to come, when the Lord, who is blessed, pays the righteous their reward, the righteous man will ask: ' Why do I get such a reward?' and it will be said unto him: ' Because thou performedst such and such a good deed on such and such a day.' Whereupon he will sigh, saying: ' For such a small thing I get such a great reward! Woe to the days that I wasted, in which I did not occupy myself with good deeds.' The wise man should therefore take heed not to waste an hour of his life, but should occupy himself with good deeds, and continually meditate in the fear of the Lord and in His service.

[10] 'Arakin 16b.

XXXV. KALONYMOS B.
KALONYMOS B. MEIR

[Satirical writer and philosopher. He was born at Arles in 1286, and died in the first half of the fourteenth century. He lived for some time in Rome, and acquired fame as an original writer and translator. His best known works are *Eben Bohan* (Stone of Investigation) and *Masseket Purim.* The former, written in rhymed prose, and modelled to some extent after Jedaiah ha-Bedersi's *Behinat 'Olam,* is a sharp criticism of the author himself and of his contemporaries, while the latter is an extremely clever parody of the Talmud. He also translated scientific books into Hebrew.]

Admonitions To His Heart [1]

O my heart, draw nigh, I pray thee; keep silence, and hearken; consider my meditation; know and discern the coming out of my words; give ear to my sayings. Shalt thou never observe the covenant? shalt thou be like an adamant harder than flint? and shalt thou not take the flint of the testimony to cut off thy foreskin and to remove thy reproach? [2] If in the days of delight and in the time of good will thy ways are unstable, what will happen when the end is come upon thee? The days of evil shall rise against thee to destroy thee; thou shalt be driven forth from the midst of men; in solitude shalt thou dwell, deserted and forsaken. What will become of thy dreams? Thou wilt be grieved for the former days that were better, and wilt groan at thy latter end.

O my heart, consider, hearken unto this. Knowest thou not that youth lasts not forever, and that the end

[1] Part of *Eben Bohan,* Venice edition, p. 59d.
[2] Comp. Exodus 4.25 and Isaiah 8.16.

of man is to die? A brother cannot redeem, none has power, and the riches of the gold of Sheba and the heights of the mountains profit not. Even if I ascend up into the heaven, and make my bed in Sheol, I shall never be able to redeem my life from destruction. Behold, a day is coming, a day of vengeance and a year of recompense, in which He will fill me with bitterness. There is no escape, for the snares of death will overtake me within the straits. As for Him who tries the hearts, His eyelids will on that day try the open and secret deeds of the children of men.

O my heart, turn round, and seek thy God within thee. It is enough for thee to reveal thyself as one of the vain fellows. Turn behind thee, for there is still hope now. Thou shalt again dwell in tents as in the days of the solemn feast, settled in a pleasant place. Fear God, and keep His commandments which are enjoined upon thee. If thou seekest Him, God will be gracious unto thee; it is from Him that thy fruit is found, the fruit which He gives according to thy deeds. Perform good deeds while thy mind is at ease, thy body fresh, and thy constitution, not lacking the right proportion, abides under the shadow of good health. It is within thy power to lift up the curtain, so that the cloud may be consumed. Look upon thy weapons wherewith thou doest thy work, thy quiver and thy bow; the strength and the blood of the body are thy rod and thy staff; in them lies the stability of thy fortune; thou shalt find them when thou seekest them; none among them is perverse or crooked.

O my heart, be strong and of good courage while the freshness of youth yet lasts: the tree of knowledge is yet in its greenness, its leaves are not scattered, and the twin-leaf is not divided; before old age strips me of the coat of youth, and sets me naked and bare ; before ' the one that departeth and cometh not back ' [3] will be taken away from me; while the cord that fell unto me in pleasantness is not yet loosed, and before the golden bowl is broken ; before the pure pieces of gold are changed, and before the wheel which turns about in the world by the command of the Almighty on high is broken. Then shall follow days of terror, during which the half-dead and feeble will not die for a month or for some years. But it shall happen one day that we shall awake and see that we were like unto them that dream.

O my heart, if not now, when shall I seek rest for me ? Shall I do it in the days of hoary hair, when the strength fails ? The branch of all mortals shall wither ; even the tender and delicate shall be dried up and wither when they grow old ; their skin shall shrivel. Will God create a new thing in me, that I may have youth after I have grown old ? Behold, I was formed out of clay ; nature fashioned me small in my dimensions ; I have the face of a man, not the face of an eagle that renews its youth at the time of old age. Moreover, I am of contrite spirit ; to my disadvantage, I was different from the young men my companions. In my youth, without old age and without mature years, I almost grew old and became grey. My strength was enfeebled as that of a woman. My senses grew weak, my thoughts became deranged, and yet I was not advanced in years. My face was wrinkled before my time, and my skin was dried up, so that it became like furrows. My head which, while in its freshness, was as the most fine gold, and upon which brown hair was grown, has white branches now, because hoariness,

[3] That is, Youth. Comp. Shabbat 152a.

snowing in its midst, is scattered over it.   In the prime of my life, while still in its full strength, my hair was plucked and torn out, and was moved out of its place. Shall my stature, which was like a palm-tree, and my back, which was straighter than a hedge, now be bowed down as a rush, so that none can raise it?   My locks, which were curly and intertwined, fall out and are scattered.   The tresses of my head, which were desirable as gold, and the hair thereof which was like purple, has become scanty, and through its departure has left breaches.   What shall I do when God arises to seek my iniquity; for behold, my sins shall surely be found.

XXXVI. LEVI B. GERSHON

[Philosopher, biblical commentator, mathematician, and physician. He is commonly called Gersonides, and is also known as Leon of Bagnols. He was born at Bagnols in 1288, and died in 1344. He was exceedingly versatile, and displayed keen originality in all branches. His best known works are his commentaries and his philosophic book *Milhamot ha-Shem* (Battles of the Lord).]

The Difficulties in Investigating the Problem Whether the Universe Is Created or Eternal [1]

It behooves us first of all to point out the great difficulty of this investigation, as this will lead us to some extent to make the investigation into this problem more complete. For by being aware of the difficulty of a problem, we are guided to the way which leads us to the attainment of the truth thereof.

The fact that the philosophers who have hitherto investigated it greatly differ from one another in their opinions concerning it points to its difficulty; for this proves that arguments may be derived from the nature of existing things, wherewith each of the conflicting views can be either established or refuted. And it is very difficult to investigate a problem with such a peculiarity.

What undoubtedly points to the great difficulty inherent in this enquiry is the fact that we have to investigate whether all existing things were created by God, who is blessed, after a period of non-existence, or were never created at all. Now it is manifest that if we desire to fathom one of the attributes of an

[1] *Milhamot ha-Shem,* part VI, chapters 1 and 2.

object, by the way of speculative investigation, whether
that object possesses that attribute or not, it is first of
all necessary that we should know the essence of the
object and its attributes. For it is only through them
that we may attain to that which we seek to know.
It is thus evident that one who desires to investigate
this problem thoroughly must first of all know the
essence and attributes of the thing under examination as far as it is possible for man to perceive. This
would necessitate that a man desirous of thoroughly
investigating this subject should know the nature and
the attributes of all existing things, so that he may be
able to explain whether there is among them a thing
or an attribute which would lead us to the conclusion
that the universe was not created; or whether there is
among them a thing or an attribute which would lead
us to the conclusion that the universe was created; or
whether there is not among them a thing or an attribute
from which it could be concluded either that the universe was created, or that it was not created. The
matter being so, a man, to whom the knowledge of one
of the existing things or of the attributes thereof, so
far as a human being can possibly know, is inaccessible,
is unable to make as thorough an investigation of this
problem as is humanly possible. Now it is evident that
to obtain as thorough a knowledge of all existing things
and of their attributes as is humanly possible is extremely difficult.

What makes this investigation more difficult is the
fact that the investigator must necessarily have
some knowledge of the First Cause as far as it is possible. For this enquiry leads him to investigate whether
God, who is blessed, could possibly have existed at first
without this world, which He afterwards brought into

existence and created, or it is necessary that the world
should have always existed with Him. It is, however,
evident from the preceding argument itself that it is
necessary for a man, desirous of making this investigation as perfect as possible, to know of the essence of
God, who is blessed, all that can be attained, so that
he may be able to decide accurately whether God, who
is blessed, can possibly be active at one time, and cease
to be active at another time, or whether this is impossible. This greatly adds to the difficulty of this investigation, since our knowledge of the essence of the
First Cause is necessarily slight, as has become manifest from the preceding.

Another point which makes this investigation still
more difficult is the circumstance that it is hard to know
from which essences or attributes of existing things it is
possible for us to attain to the truth of this problem.
For it is necessary that a man, desirous of making this
investigation perfect, should know this at the very out-
set, otherwise he can only attain to the truth thereof
by accident.

The statement of the philosopher,[2] as recorded by the
author of the *Guide,* points to the difficulty of this investigation. It is as follows: ' As for the things concerning which we have no argument, and which are
too high for us, our statement about them is, according to this, as difficult as our statement whether the
world is eternal or not.'[3] This shows that this question was considered extremely difficult by the philosopher, so that he was perplexed and doubtful about it,
despite the numerous arguments he mentioned to prove
that the universe is eternal. The reason for that is

[2] That is, Aristotle.
[3] *Guide of the Perplexed,* book II, chapter 15. The quotation
is inaccurate.

undoubtedly because the philosopher assumed that there were numerous arguments likewise to prove that the universe was created, and that his own arguments did not in any way establish the truth in this matter; and this is the very truth, as will be explained further on. Now if this question was considered difficult by the philosopher, despite his high rank of wisdom, how much more difficult would it be to other men who are lower than he on the ladder of knowledge.

And indeed we find that the opinions of the ancients concerning this investigation are diametrically opposed to one another. Some maintain that the universe was created and destroyed an endless number of times. Others hold that it was created only once; these are divided into two opinions: some of them think that the universe was created out of something, as, for instance, Plato and the later philosophers who follow his doctrine; while others think that the universe was created out of absolute non-existence, as for instance the early Mutakallimites, like Yahya the grammarian, according to what Ibn Rushd recorded of him in his commentary on the *Metaphysics*. In this theory they were followed by the Mutakallimites. This view was also adopted by the great philosopher, the author of the *Guide*, and by many of the sages of our religion. But there are still others who maintain that the universe is eternal. This is the theory of the philosopher and his followers. It is evident that the cause of their disagreement concerning these doctrines is the variety of objects from which they derived their proofs with regards to the nature of existing things, or because they were compelled by the Torah, or because of these two causes combined.

XXXVII. PROFIAT DURAN

[Philosopher and grammarian. He is called Maestre Profiat
and Efodi, but his Hebrew name was Isaac b. Moses ha-Levi.
He was born in the second half of the fourteenth century, and
lived for some time in Perpignan. During the persecutions in
1391 he was an ostensible convert to Christianity. He afterwards wrote an epistle entitled *Al Tehi ka-Aboteka* (Be not
like thy Fathers) in which he attacked Christianity in such a
manner that the superficial reader may take it as a eulogy on
that religion. His best work is his philosophic-critical Hebrew
grammar entitled *Ma'aseh Efod*. It is so called because the
letters אפֿד are the initials of אני פריפוט דוראן.]

The Definition of the Science of Language and Its Branches [1]

The science of language is a science comprising
grammar, rhetoric, and poetry. It is therefore fitting
that its definition should be given in a manner that
harmonizes with these three branches, and afterwards
each of them should be differentiated by its specific
characteristic. I say that the science of language is
a science which teaches the general methods that may
be employed in a language, in a manner fitting the
conventionalities of that language. By saying: 'In
a manner fitting' I wish to convey that the expression must agree with that which is conceived by the
mind, according to the linguistic axioms. I call the
study of language a science, because the term 'science'
is indeed more comprehensive than the philosophers
think. For they have defined science as an acquisition
which the mind attains by true beginnings and causes;
by 'true beginnings' they mean the beginnings which

[1] *Ma'aseh Efod,* chapter 8, pp. 42, *seq.*

are known either through the nature of the intellect, as the first principles, or through sense perception, or through experience. According to this, the study of language is no science at all, for its beginnings are conventional, and are not evolved through any of the ways that I have mentioned. In our opinion, however, the term 'science' is more comprehensive, for we call science anything that is known through investigation, analogy, or proof, no matter whether the principles and beginnings upon which it is based are essentially true, or arbitrary and conventional. The teacher [2] has already called such sciences 'conventional sciences.' Accordingly, the study of language is a science, and the definition of science rightly applies to it; for by it are known, through investigation and proof, the results derived from principles and beginnings which have been laid down in it. The wise man R. Jonah said in the description of grammar that it signifies investigation and searching. This is merely an interpretation of the term, which does not give us the definition of grammar itself.

Now when a speech is merely in conformity with the principles and rules of the language, without having sweetness, beauty, polish, and embellishment, in the simple and complex forms, and is not free from superfluity or excessive brevity compared with the meaning intended to be conveyed, such a discourse is said to be merely grammatical; the man who essentially and constantly speaks in that manner is said to be a grammarian; and the power by which he speaks in that manner is called grammar. When the speech also has sweetness, beauty, polish, and embellishment, in the simple and complex forms, it is said to be rhetorical

[2] That is, Maimonides.

(it is derived from the expression: 'How sweet are Thy words unto my palate!' [3] which signifies: how sweet and pleasant are they!); the author of such a speech is called a rhetorician, provided that this manner of speech is essential and constant with him; and the capacity which he has for such a speech is called rhetoric. If in addition to all these characteristics, the speech is also metrical, it is called a poem; its author is called a poet, provided this is essential and constant with him; and the capacity which he possesses for that is called poetry. By the word 'metre' I mean to say that the portions of the discourse are equal in the number of their vowels (thou already knowest about that). This is called a poem, because by means of the metre it is possible to sing it aloud. The term 'poem' has also been applied to anything that is to be understood allegorically, as, for instance, the Song of Songs, and others. The rhetorical discourses and poems of the Jews have a special characteristic which I have not seen or heard in the discourses and poems of other nations. The Jewish rhetoricians and poets add sweetness, beauty, and polish to their sentences by giving their rhetorical discourses and poems the form of the scriptural verses and of the sayings of the wise and by their endeavoring that that form should agree with the meaning of their discourses, either according to the plain meaning of the Bible, or according to some figurative application which they put into the discourse. It is the highest degree of elegance and beauty in rhetoric and rhetoricians when they make their discourses to be in harmony with, and add to them sweetness from, the divine speech. This is due to the circumstance

[3] Psalm 119. 103.

that the Hebrew tongue is now deficient, as was explained, and therefore the rhetoricians, when they wish to render their discourses sweet and elegant, find it necessary to embellish and beautify them with the rhetorical expressions that exist. Accordingly, their loss is cancelled by their gain, and their deficiency turned to advantage. I have likewise noticed that the Jewish rhetoricians possess another peculiarity not shared by the rhetoricians of other nations : the knowledge of grammar comes to them naturally, and their discourses are always in conformity with the principles and rules of the science of language, though they do not study the books that were composed on this science ; yet it is only casually, and very rarely, that they commit mistakes or errors according to the principles of the language. One is not to condemn or to blame them for that, for even in the works of nature casual mistakes are sometimes found. This power of theirs with which they were endowed by nature caused them to neglect and disregard the study of the books devoted to the science of language, which are accounted by them as things of nought and confusion.

14

XXXVIII. SIMON B. ZEMAH DURAN

[Rabbinical authority and philosopher. He was born at the island of Majorca in 1361, and died in 1444. He lived for some time in Algiers. His literary activity was devoted to philosophy, Bible, and Talmud, and his best known work is *Magen Abot* (Shield of the Fathers), which is a theological-philosophical treatise.]

On the Problem Why the Wicked Prosper and the Righteous Are in Distress [1]

Indeed the difficulty about the wicked man who is prosperous seems to be no difficulty at all. For God, who is blessed, is good, and bestows good upon all. He does not withhold good from the wicked, just as He does not withhold from the lions their claws wherewith they tear their prey, for they are needed for the acquisition of their food. In all this the philosopher and the theologian concur; there is no difference between them. The only difference between them is that the philosopher cannot believe that divine Providence should attach itself to an individual, to save him from evils for his righteousness, or to withhold bliss from him for his wickedness; while the theologian believes that Providence attaches itself to an individual just as it attaches itself to the entire species which is permanent. For an individual man's intellect is as permanent as the species, and hence Providence attaches itself to him, just as it attaches itself to the species. There is a very subtle speculation in this. For it is known that the species exist only in the intellect, and that nothing

<hr>

[1] *Magen Abot,* part 3, chapter 2, p. 33.

210

but individuals actually exist. Aristotle, however, in his *Metaphysics* has explained that the matter is quite the reverse, that the individuals create the species in their intellects, through repetition.[2] Now since the species have no actual existence, and Providence can only attach itself to that which has actual existence, what is the cause of their permanence according to the philosopher? For he is of the opinion that Providence attaches itself only to that which has permanence, and the species is the only thing that has permanence; but the species has no existence, and Providence cannot attach itself to that which has no existence. He therefore says that Providence is confined to the spheres, stars, and separate intelligences, and that the species are preserved through the influence that emanates from them to this mental existence. But as to individuals, all their affairs are abandoned to chance, there being no difference between individuals of the human race and the individuals of animals. The theologian, however, believes that divine Providence attaches itself to individuals on account of their intellect, although it has not the same permanence as the separate intelligences and as the intellect of the spheres. All that is found in this lower world was created for the use of man. Accordingly, from Providence that is attached to each individual man there emanates a Providence to the species of the animals, so that through their preservation the existence of man should be preserved. Upon this matter the philosophers are agreed; when they have investigated the functions of the limbs and the functions of the animals, vegetables, and minerals, they have found them all to be for the benefit of man, either for his food, raiment,

[2] That is, through repetition of perception.

sustenance, and dwelling-place, or for curing his dis-
eases. For even in harmful things there may be
found a cure and some benefit for man. If a pious
man has sometimes been cured with the excrement
of a devouring lion, or with the skin of a venomous
snake, then that injurious thing was created for the
benefit of man. Similarly, if one planted a vineyard,
and made wine which a pious man has drunk when
stung by a viper and has been cured thereby, then
that wine was created for the benefit of that pious
man. In a similar manner our saintly teacher [3] said,
when he was cured of an illness by apple-cider seventy
years old that was in the possession of a Gentile:
' Blessed be He who handed over His world to custo-
dians.' It is likewise for this reason that our sages
of blessed memory said: ' The Holy One, blessed be
He, has only four cubits of the law in His world.' [4]
They likewise said: ' The entire world was created
to attend to man.' [5] Ben Zoma said: ' Blessed be He
who created all these to serve me.' [6] Concerning all this
I have already written in a preceding chapter. Now it
is impossible that all this is by mere chance, and is, therefore, due to divine Providence, as I shall, with the help
of God, explain at full length, when treating of the soul.

A strong argument is urged by the theologian against
the philosopher in this connection. Since man's intellect is as permanent as the angels, divine Providence ought to attach itself to the intellect, as it attaches itself to the angels. Moreover, this fact made
itself manifest to the senses, as Scripture relates
of the punishment of the wicked, that some times

[3] That is, Rabbi Judah ha-Nasi. See 'Abodah Zarah 40b.
[4] Berakot 8a.
[5] Ibid. 6b; Shabbat 30b.
[6] Berakot 58a.

hyperphysical and supernatural calamities befall them, having been forewarned by a man renowned as a prophet ; at the same time the righteous are delivered from these calamities, and prosper against the laws of nature. This cannot be attributed to chance and accident, for it occurred very frequently, and the warning had been given by a man sent by God, who is blessed, whose message could not be doubted. With all these arguments the theologian establishes his belief that God, who is blessed, supervises every individual of the human race, giving a goodly reward to the righteous, and bringing calamities upon the wicked.

To this the philosopher replies and says that, had the affairs of the world been arranged in this manner, the contention of the theologians would have been justified. But we also see that supernatural calamities befall many righteous men, and, on the other hand, many of the wicked who deserve evil prosper in a manner contrary to natural reason. Had things been arranged by God, who is blessed, as the theologian maintains, the righteous man should have been delivered from the misfortunes which had befallen him, and prosperity should have been withheld from the wicked.

The theologian says with regard to the misfortunes that have come upon the righteous that it is a fallacious contention. The fallacy is due to one of two considera · tions : either on account of the subject, or on account of the object. As to the subject, it is possible that this man who, according to all appearances, is righteous, is not good at all ; for He who understands his secrets knows that he is bad ; men are deceived about him, and decide that he is good, but He who understands his thoughts knows him to be bad. Or he may have committed a crime for which he deserves this calamity. As to the object, it is possible that these occurrences which appear to be bad are not bad at all, but are for the good of the sufferer.

In this manner the theologian evades the philosopher's objection with reference to the righteous upon whom misfortunes have come, and this ramifies into many details. As to the prosperity of the wicked, the theologian likewise says that there is a fallacy due to one of two considerations: either on account of the subject, or on account of the object. As to the subject, it is possible that this wicked man, although his deeds committed openly show him to be undoubtedly bad, must have performed a good deed for which he deserves this prosperity as a recompense. As to the object, it is possible that this prosperity is for his own harm. This, too, is a general argument having many ramifications with which the theologian evades the objection with reference to the wicked who is prosperous.

XXXIX. JOSEPH ALBO

[Spanish theologian and philosopher. He was born about 1380, and died about 1444. His philosophic treatise entitled *'Ikkarim* (Principles) is one of the great favorites of Hebrew readers. He has a clear style, and makes himself readily understood. It is no doubt due to this characteristic that he supplanted his master Hisdai Crescas, author of *Or ha-Shem* (Light of the Lord).]

The Various Ranks of Prophecy [1]

Although all the words of the prophets are doubtless true, nevertheless the degree of the exactitude of a prophet's words corresponds to his rank and degree in prophecy. There are many prophets who, because of the weakness of their perception, do not perceive things with sufficient clarity. For that which happens to the perceptions of the senses happens also to the perceptions of the prophets: a man whose senses are healthy and strong perceives objects in their exact form, while one whose senses are feeble does not perceive them in their exact form, and perceives only their species, or their genus, without being able to distinguish the species. Thus a man with a strong sense of sight recognizes a color, which he preceives, as it actually is (as, for instance, red or green); he likewise recognizes the degree of redness or greenness. But one whose sense of sight is weak recognizes only the genus, that is to say, that it is a color, and no more; and even if he recognizes the species, that is to say, that it is red or green, he does not know what degree of redness or greenness it is. The same is the case with the sense of hearing and with the other

[1] *'Ikkarim,* part 3, chapter 17.

215

senses. This very thing happens to the prophets as regards their perception. One whose perception is strong perceives the thing as it actually is without a metaphor; his words are explicit, not obscure, and are therefore to be understood as true according to their plain meaning. But the words of a prophet of a lower degree are obscure, couched in riddles and parables, and are not explicit; they are therefore not true according to their plain meaning, but only according to the idea implied in them; for according to the literal sense, something else, different from that which is conveyed by the words, is to be understood. Thou thus findest that Ezekiel, his prophecies being post-exilic, spoke in parables and riddles which were not true according to their plain meaning, so that he complained of this to God, who is blessed, and said: ' They say of me: " Is he not a maker of parables? " ' [2] Zechariah, likewise, having flourished toward the end of the prophetic period, all his prophecies were in visions which were not true according to their plain meaning, but only according to that which was implied in them. When he says that he saw horses, women, and a golden candlestick with two olive-trees by it, there is no truth in the matter of the candlestick and olive-trees itself, but only in the idea implied in them. But all the prophecies of Jeremiah, who lived before the destruction of the temple, are very clearly explained. God, who is blessed, has already explained this difference between the prophecy of Moses and that of another prophet. Concerning the prophecy of Moses He said: ' I speak with him mouth to mouth, even manifestly, and not in dark speeches.' [3]   From

[2] Ezekiel 21. 5.
[3] Numbers 12. 8.

this it is to be inferred that the other prophets beside Moses speak in riddles which are not explicit, and in visions which are not real. It is therefore necessary that these visions should be explained in such a manner that they harmonize with Moses' words. Similarly, the words of a prophet of a lower rank should always be explained in such a manner that they harmonize with the words of a prophet of a higher rank and do not dissent from him. It is in accordance with this explanation that we find that Isaiah says: ' And I saw the Lord sitting upon a throne, high and lifted up,'[4] while Moses says: 'For man shall not see Me and live.'[5] Had we not known the rank of either of these prophets, we might have thought Isaiah's words were accurate, and would have said that because of his high rank he perceived of God that which can possibly be perceived of Him, and he therefore said: 'And I saw the Lord;' but Moses, who did not reach Isaiah's rank, and perceived but little of God, said: 'For man shall not see Me and live,' because his perception was weak, and his prophetic rank low. Knowing, however, that Moses was master of all prophets (as it is written: 'And the Lord spoke unto Moses face to face, as a man speaketh unto his friend,'[6] and it is likewise written: 'If there be a prophet among you, I the Lord do make Myself known unto him in a vision, I do speak with him in a dream; My servant Moses is not so. . . . . With him do I speak mouth to mouth, even manifestly, and not in dark speeches'[7]), we are assured that Moses' words are undoubtedly true according to their plain mean-

[4] Isaiah 6. 1.
[5] Exodus 33. 20.
[6] Exodus 33. 11.
[7] Numbers 12. 6-8.

ing. On the other hand, the words of Isaiah, who was lower than he in rank, are not accurate; it is because of his low rank that he said: ' And I saw the Lord; ' for he believed that he saw God, while it was not so in reality: it was through the influence of the imaginative faculty. Moses, however, because the imaginative faculty had no influence whatsoever on his prophecy (for his prophecy was the outcome of the rational faculty that was in him, detached from the other corporeal faculties), said: ' For man shall not see Me and live; ' and this is true. But Isaiah, because in his prophecy he also made use of the imaginative faculty, which our teachers of blessed memory call ' the speculum which is not lucid,'[8] was led to err and to believe, through the imaginative faculty, that he had seen God. He himself made it manifest that this perception of his was erroneous, through the imaginative faculty, and explained that the cause thereof was that his body was not purified as the body of Moses our teacher; and that is the meaning of what he said: ' Because I am a man of unclean lips.'[9] Nor were his qualities adequate; and that is the meaning of what he said: ' And I dwell in the midst of a people of unclean lips.'[10] For through dwelling among people of bad traits, the qualities of the good man become corrupt. He therefore complained, and said: ' Woe is me! for I am undone,'[11] as if he would say: ' I was influenced by the imaginative faculty, and my prophecy is not through a lucid speculum like the prophecy of Moses who heard the voice speaking to him, without seeing any form before

[8] Yebamodt 49b.
[9] Isaiah 6. 5.
[10] *Ibid.*
[11] *Ibid.* In the Hebrew the word for *undone* is similar to the one for *imaginative.*

his eyes. But I, because my prophecy is through a speculum which is not lucid, that is by means of the imaginative faculty, I am not able to comprehend the speech without seeing the form that is speaking. This was caused by my being a man of unclean lips, and by my dwelling in the midst of a people of unclean lips. I therefore complain, and say: Woe is me! for I am undone. For my eyes have seen the King, the Lord of hosts, and I know that this is the result of the imaginative faculty; since there is no doubt that it is impossible for one who prophesies through the lucid speculum to attribute any form or likeness to Him, who is blessed, even in a prophetic vision.' This is the meaning of what our sages of blessed memory said: ' Manasseh slew Isaiah. Whereupon Raba says: He tried him and slew him. He said unto him: Thy master Moses said: For man shall not see Me and live, but thou didst say: And I saw the Lord.' [12] They have also remarked that he could have refuted this argument, but he did not reply, because he knew that Manasseh would not accept his answer. The answer that he could have given is that even concerning those that lived in the time of Moses it is written: ' And they saw the God of Israel; ' [13] here, too, because their perception was not through the lucid speculum. From all this it is manifest that it is not possible for a prophet of a lower rank to dissent from the words of one who is of a higher rank; but his words must be explained in such a manner that they are not at variance with the words of the greater prophet. Now, since it is explicitly stated in the Torah that Moses' prophecy is of a rank higher than that of all other

[12] Yebamot 49b.
[13] Exodus 24. 10.

prophets, it is not possible for us to hearken to any prophet who dissents from him, and annuls his words. But the question whether it is possible for a prophet to explain the words of Moses, and to say that, although they were written without a qualification, there is a condition or time connected with them, even if it was not explicitly stated, will be treated of in the following, with the help of God.

XL. ISAAC B. JUDAH ABRAVANEL

[Statesman, philosopher, and biblical exegete. He was born at Lisbon in 1437, and died at Venice in 1508. He was treasurer at the court of king Alfonso V of Portugal. When the Jews were expelled from Spain, he left that country and went to Naples. He was a prolific writer, and in all his works he displayed clear-sightedness and a thorough mastery of the subjects under discussion, though he lacked striking originality. His most popular work is his commentary on the Bible.]

The Advantages of a Republic over a Monarchy [1]

Behold, it behooves us to know whether a monarch is a necessity, inherently needed for the people, or it is possible to exist without him. The philosophers adopt the former opinion, and think that the service rendered by the king to the people in the political organization is the same as the relation of the heart to the body in animals possessing a heart, and as the relation of the First Cause to the entire universe. Now if the investigators think that a kingdom must be based on three things (firstly, unity and absence of partnership; secondly, continuity and absence of change; thirdly, absolute power), then their conclusion as to the need and necessity of a monarch is indeed fallacious. For it is not impracticable that a people should have many leaders, united, agreeing, and concurring in one counsel, who should decide administrative and judicial matters. This militates against the first principle. Then, why should not their administration be for one year, or for three years, like the years of a hireling, or less than that?

[1] Commentary on Deuteronomy 17. 15.

When the turn of other judges and officers comes, they will arise in their stead, and investigate whether the first ones have not failed in their trust, and he whom they condemn shall make good the wrong he committed. This militates against the second principle. Then again, why should not their power be limited and regulated according to the laws and statutes? A common-sense principle tells us that when one man disagrees with the majority, the law is according to the majority. It is more likely that one man should trespass, through his folly, or strong temptations or anger (as it is written: 'the wrath of a king is as messengers of death'[2]), than that many men taking counsel should transgress. For if one of them turns aside from the right path, the others will protest against him. Moreover, since their administration is temporary, and they must render account after a short while, the fear of man will be upon them. But what need is there of producing abstract arguments, since experience is more forceful than logic? Behold and see the countries where the administration is in the hands of kings, and you will observe their abominations and corruptions, every one of them does that which is right in his own eyes; for the earth is filled with wickedness through them. On the other hand, we see this day many countries where the administration is in the hands of judges; temporary rulers are elected there, and over them is a chief against whom there is no rising up; they choose that which is right by definite regulations; they rule over the people, and decide concerning matters appertaining to war; none can withstand them, whether it be for the rod or for the land.'

[2] Proverbs 16. 14.
[3] Comp. Job 37. 13.

Dost thou not know? hast thou not heard that there was a great country that had dominion over all the world? She devoured the whole earth, trod it down, and broke it in pieces, when her administration was in the hands of the numerous consuls, who were faithful, numerous, and held temporary offices. But after an emperor was made to rule over it, it became tributary. Even to-day Venice rules as a mistress, great among nations, a princess among the states, and the state of Florence is the glory of all lands. There are likewise other states, great and small, which have no king, and are governed by leaders elected for a fixed time. Now in the elected governments in which there is nothing crooked or perverse, no man lifts his hand or his foot to commit any matter of trespass. They conquer countries with wisdom, understanding, and knowledge. All this proves that the existence of a monarch is not necessary; nay, it it harmful, and is a great danger. In a similar manner the author of the *Guide* [4] warned against the great dangers incurred in travelling on the seas and in serving kings, on account of the similarity that exists between the two in the possibility of danger, both being alike, the stormy wind on the ocean and the spirit of the ruler. It is surprising that the adherents of that erroneous opinion have compared the unity of a king elected by the authority and will of men to the unity of the First Cause, who is blessed, the necessarily eternal. Indeed the wise men have written concerning the body of an animal that there are three vital members which control it. Even according to the opinion of the chief of the philosophers that the heart is the only vital member, this merely refers to the production of the spirit; but he does

[4] That is, Maimonides.

not deny the control of the body by the other faculties, by the psychical, which are from the brain, and the physical which are from the liver. To conclude, things of nature are inevitably arrayed in this manner, but those which result from the action of the will belong to the category of the contingent. The one cannot be compared to the other.

No oojection can be raised from the saying: 'For the transgression of a land many are the princes thereof;'[5] for that verse speaks of the princes, not of the leaders and the judges. How can we ignore self-evident facts? For if the leaders are good, it is better that they should be many and not one; if they are bad, one left free to his lusts is more dangerous than many.

I therefore think that kings were at first set up to rule not by the people's elections, but by force: the one that was stronger prevailed; as it is written: 'Let us go up against Judah, and vex it, and set up a king in the midst of it.'[6] Even these were only appointed as a matter of trust, to serve the people; but they made themselves masters, as if God, who is blessed, gave them the earth and the fulness thereof, and they leave it as an inheritance to their children after them and to their children's children for ever, as if it were a plot of land which one acquires for money. This cursed plague has spread so much that sometimes a man arises, and rules alone, and governs according to his imagination. This, however, is not alike in all kingdoms; for in some of them the king does not have so much power in the administration. But the better of the two is the one that does not yet exist.

[5] Proverbs 28. 2.
[6] Isaiah 7. 6 (shortened).

XLI. SOLOMON IBN VERGA

[Spanish historian and physician who flourished during the fifteenth and sixteenth centuries. He was compelled to flee to Turkey, where he wrote his *Shebet Yehudah* (Rod of Judah), which gives an account of the Jewish persecutions in various countries. This book is valuable for Jewish folk-lore, though not always trustworthy as a historical source.]

A Jew Is Accused of Murdering a Christian, But His Innocence Is Proved [1]

In the time of the righteous king Alfonso the Elder, some men came before the judges of the country, and related that they had seen a Christian enter the house of a Jew on the eve of Passover, and subsequently heard him exclaim, saying: ' Save me, O Christians! ' The judges then sent some men, who went to search in the house of the Jew; but they did not find anything. Whereupon the judges said: ' A similar accusation was made last year, but the falsehood thereof became apparent. Now, ye accusers, why do ye walk after vanity, and why do ye harass these poor people, although there is no violence in their hands? ' The people arose with an uproarious sound, and said: ' Shall not the judge of all the land do right? We shall go to the king, for he will bring our judgment to light.'

When they came before the king, and related the whole affair to him, the king said: ' Bring that Jew before me.' The Jew was immediately brought before him, and when questioned by the king, he replied:

[1] *Shebet Yehudah,* 29, Wiener's edition, pp. 48, *seq.*

'Far be it from me! for no Christian entered my
house for some time.' The king then said to the
accusers: 'Ye deserve death. When ye heard the
Christian exclaim, saying: "Save me!", and ye
recognized his voice, why did ye not break the doors
of the Jew's house, and enter there to save the op-
pressed from the hand of the oppressor?' They
replied that they were afraid of the judges, lest they
should fine them for breaking another man's door.
Whereupon the Jew remarked: 'But how is it that
ten days ago, when a slave ran away, and entered my
house, where he locked himself up, ye broke my doors,
which have not been repaired yet?' So they withdrew
in silence, without answering a word. Whereupon
the king said to the lords: 'Have you seen the Jew
the Christian-killer? He is very old and decrepit,
has not the strength to kill a fly. It is all on account
of the wickedness of the hearts of these men who
deserve to be punished.' He then turned his face to
them, and said: 'Ye are falsifiers and liars. Take
heed unto yourselves that ye come not again with such
a thing before me.'

On the second day they assembled, and came again
to the king, saying that there were many witnesses
and strong evidence. Whereupon the king said:
'Since it is so, it is necessary to make an investigation.' He commanded that the king's scribe should
come. The latter came, and wrote down the name of
the Jew and the sign of his house. He also inquired
of that Christian's acquaintances, who claimed to
have known him, what his name was. They said it
was Pedro Guzman. He asked about his wife, and
they said that she was Beatrice the attendant of the
bishop and that she lived in such and such a street. The

king then asked: ' What is the description of the Christian?', and they replied: ' A young man of short stature, ruddy, with parted beard, and blind of one eye.' The king sent for the woman, and asked her concerning her husband. She said: ' He went to the house of a Jew to collect money which the Jew owed him, but has not yet returned to my house.' After that the king asked for the testimony of the young men, and they said: ' That Christian, whose descriptions were such and such, was our acquaintance. We met him at the door of the Jew, and he told us that he was waiting for the Jew on account of a debt which the Jew owed him. While we were still talking, the Jew came, and the Christian entered the house with him. A little while later we heard the Christian's voice, crying: " Save me." Whereupon we entered the Jew's house through the window, and searched all over, but did not find the Christian. We, however, found a large quantity of blood upon the ground.' The king then said: ' According to this evidence he deserves to be tortured.' So they beat the Jew, until he confessed that he had killed the Christian and thrown him into the river at night. Whereupon he was condemned to be burned.

During the reading of the sentence the archbishop came before the king. Having listened to the reading of the sentence, the bishop asked: ' Is this Pedro de Guzman the husband of Beatrice, or another man?' They replied: ' The husband of Beatrice.' The bishop then said: ' I observe astonishing things here. The sentence says that the Jew killed him on the first of January, but I met him alive last night in a village near the city; he will return to-day or to-morrow.' Whereupon the king said: ' In this case, either the Jew was mad, or has just lost his senses, for he has confessed to a crime which he did not commit.' But the bishop said: 'No trust, nor reliance is to be placed in torture or in the acts of the lords.' The Jew said: 'Our lord the king! I am not mad, nor have I ever been mad; but they made me lose my senses through torture; for mercy has perished from the Christians, and they executed on me such judgments as are not executed on those who rebel against the king's crown. Seeing that after inflicting many kinds of torture, they kept on devising new ones, I preferred one death to several deaths.'

The king then sent two of his servants to bring the Christian, and he also sent a Jew with them, in order that they should not bribe him and hide him. When the Christian came before the king, the king stood up on his feet, and said: 'Praised be He who sheds light upon obscure things! Praised be He to whom belongeth justice and judgment! Why did He charge fools like us to sit upon the throne of justice, while we are like the beasts of the field that know not at what they stumble? Moreover, I heard that in ancient times it had been the custom of the Greeks to weep when an infant was born, and to rejoice and laugh when an old man died. Their reason was because it is fitting to weep for the new-born babe, since he is come to the valley of weeping; but when he dies, it is fitting to rejoice, since he has gone to a place of rejoicing and rest. Now the Jews ought to weep when they are born and when they die, as well as during the days that intervene; for it is not enough that they suffer evils inherent in exile, but their enemies seek occasions against them to overthrow them. I grieve very much for them, not because they are

Jews, but because they are poor and lowly. We have no other kingdom, but that which the King of the universe gave us; and He said by His prophet: " But on this man will I look, even on him that is poor and of a contrite spirit." [2] Now thou, O bishop, deservest my favor, for thou hast kept me back from shedding innocent blood. The Lord sent thee, in order that perverted justice should not go forth from our hand.'

Whereupon the bishop said: ' There is yet another favor which the King, the Lord of the universe, has shown thee. For thou hast seen with thine own eyes that no trust nor reliance is to be placed in that which a man says while being beaten or tortured; for this poor Jew said that he had killed that Christian who is here standing alive before our lord. Praised be He who gives light to upright and righteous rulers like thee. May He make His face shine upon thee for ever. Amen.'

[2] Isaiah 66. 2.

XLII. ABRAHAM B. MORDECAI FERIZOL

[Scholar and geographer. He was born at Avignon in 1451, and died in the first half of the sixteenth century. Early in life he settled in Italy, and is said to have been cantor in a Ferrara synagogue. He is the first geographical writer in Hebrew. Although he wrote a number of other treatises, he is best known by his *Iggeret Orehot 'Olam* (Treatise on the Paths of the World), which is a cosmographic and geographic work.]

A Jew Who Claims to Belong to the Ten Tribes Visits Italy [1]

For the sake of the usefulness of this treatise, which I, Abraham Ferizol, have composed in order to make plain the paths of the world unto them that know not, I chose to write this chapter, the pivot of which turns upon the ways of the Jew of the ten tribes (who may possibly have been of the tribe of Judah), whose name is David the son of Solomon, a captain of the host of Israel. He came here, and we saw him in this our province, the province of Italy. I shall relate how he came from the wilderness of Habor, according to his words. In this narrative the readers will find repose for their souls, and those who are weary of desire shall rest here. For in the narrative set forth in my words I shall not deviate from what I know from the mouth of trustworthy people, and from what I saw in the writing of truthful men. And God knows the truth, because He alone is the truth; though I am one of those who put little faith in vanities.

[1] *Iggeret Orehot 'Olam,* chapter 14, Hyde's edition, pp. 90, *seq.*

This is the narrative: In the year 283 of the sixth millennium we heard tidings from the Land of Glory in a Hebrew letter which came by the way of the boats from Venice, declaring that a Jew of the ten tribes had arrived there and announced new things in the midst of the land. There is no need of these narratives, since he crossed the sea in the year 284, arrived in Venice, and went up to Rome, where he was declared as truthful by those who knew the manner and conduct of his life. As was understood from the words which he spoke, this Jew belongs to the sect of the two tribes. For he said that he was one of those who dwell in tents in the deserts, like the sons of the Rechabites, and that his dwelling-place is in the wilderness of Habor which is in Asia Major, and that lower down, on the other side, are the rest of the ten tribes. They live close to the deserts which are traversed on the way to Mecca and Jedda, which are by the Red Sea. They all have kings and princes and vast populations like the sand which is on the sea-shore. There is the origin of spices, pepper, and simple medicines, and other good products which are found in their hands, as I shall describe in its proper place. Between these two sects of Jews there is indeed a strong and mighty nation of Ishmaelites who have many kings, and do harm to the sect of these Jews, by not allowing them to go across and join their fellow-Jews. For many years they spread forth, and attempted to come near to each other, but did not succeed. But when the arrival of the strong and mighty boats of the Christians became known in these regions many years ago, and they perceived, heard of, and saw the instruments of war which are in the hands of the Christians (the hollowed metals for throwing stones by the force of fire, wherewith one can destroy all habitations and fortifications), the Jews who live in the wilderness of Habor chose to send this Jew, according to his words, to the great king of all the Christians. In order that his words may be believed, he had in his hands credentials which were verified and established by the king of Portugal who travels by means of a boat across the ocean to these Hoddian, that is Indian, regions, and knows of the existence of a Jewish kingdom there. He wrote to the pope, may his glory be exalted, that this Jew, mentioned above, was faithful, and that his words were trustworthy. At all events, it matters not whether his words are trustworthy or not, it is sufficient for us to-day in this our exile, and in our provinces, that it has been verified by kings and princes and made known in public and in the streets of Rome that the very numerous tribes of Israel still exist, and that they have many kings. As for this Jew who came here, it matters not who he is.

Since it is true that the Jews and their kings still exist, it is possible to say that this Jew came by the following route in the following manner: From the wilderness of Habor he went by the caravan pass, for this is customary, and thus was it written and heard from his mouth concerning himself. He then crossed the Pole of Arabia Felix, and came to the Red Sea, whence he came down to Egypt. Afterwards he went up to the Land of Glory, where he waited for the boats coming from Venice, that he might cross over to Italy. He then went to Rome, where he stayed about eight months until there came the reply of the king of Portugal concerning the truthfulness of his words and his affair.

The narrators and prominent Jews who spoke with him declare that this Jew really did ask the pope, the king of the Gentiles, for assistance, that instruments of war (metals for throwing stones) and skilful workers should be given to him, so that he might take them along with him to Arabia Felix to destroy their above-mentioned enemies. He would give to the pope and his office certain concessions for the benefit of the pope, may his glory be exalted, and a way to rule over some of the places where there are collectors of wealth, and spices, and simple medicines. The object of this is that these Jews may be united and gathered together to go across and take possession of the Land of Glory and subdue it, for it is an everlasting inheritance unto Israel. All this have my eyes seen in truthful letters, and my ears heard from prominent and truthful people. But the Lord God is the absolute truth, He lies not, and speaks no falsehood; they that take refuge in Him shall not be put to shame. Truth springs forth of its own accord, and makes its way.

And this day, in the month Marheshvan, in the year 285, we have heard that Pope Clement, the king of the Gentiles, spoke to him, and agreed to dismiss him and send him away by way of Portugal with honor and with a big boat full of instruments of war and of Jewish and Christian skilful workers. He also arranged with the king of Portugal to supply the Jew's needs, and commanded every Christian nation, wherever he passes through, to honor him, assist him, and fulfil his desire with regard to the requirements mentioned above. All this shall stand as it is.

Now I merely propose to describe the route by which, in my opinion, he may go more safely than by any other route, if the narrators are right. He should be taken to Portugal, and thence he should go down to the ocean, going round the coast of Fez, and proceed by sea all the way to the right of the Fortunate Isles which are now called Spain. He should then continue on dry land by way of Cape Verde, and go round Africa on dry land to the left, going eastward as far as the big Promontory, which is called Cape of Good Hope. He should then cross the Gulf of the Berbers to the outlet of the straits of the Red Sea, and go down on dry land to the outlet of the wilderness of Habor, wherever it may be, and go to his place, as I shall explain all the new outlets later on.

According to hearsay, these are the descriptions and manners of this Jew: He is of short stature, lean-fleshed, and courageous; he prays frequently, is dark-complexioned, and afflicts himself with fasting. According to the words of the writers, he could fast for six consecutive days and nights.

His principal language is the holy tongue, which he speaks almost unintelligibly, like a stammerer. Sometimes prominent men and cardinals of Rome came to visit him in his house, but he thrust them aside, and would not receive them. He rode on a mule in Rome to see the curiosities of the country, and, while on his mule, entered the great temple of St. Peter, even as far as the great altar, refusing to dismount his mule. There were with him about ten Jews running before him, and more than two hundred Christians.

May the Lord speak good concerning Israel.

XLIII. JOSEPH B. JOSHUA B. MEIR HA-KOHEN

[Historian and physician. He was born at Avignon in 1496, and died at Genoa in 1575. His best known works are *Dibre ha-Yamin le-Malke Zarefat we-'Utman,* which is a sort of history of the world, and *'Emek ha-Baka,* which deals with the Jewish persecutions in various countries and centuries. The latter book was begun in 1558, and concluded in 1563. He subsequently brought it up to 1575.]

The Crusaders Massacre the Jews at Meurs [1]

And it came to pass in the fourth month on the seventh day, that the enemies, the men of the army, arose against the poor and humble population of Meurs, and besieged the city round about. When the inhabitants of that town lifted up their eyes, they saw a people as the sand of the sea, which cannot be numbered for multitude. These people asked that the Jews should be handed over to them to do unto them according to their desire, as they had done in all the towns through which they had passed up till that day. The governor of the town went out to them, and said to the captains of the army: ' What profit is it if we slay our brethren, these Jews, who dwell in our midst in security, and conceal their blood? Therefore remain ye outside, and I shall speak in their ears, and whatever answer they will give me, I shall tell you. These men will perhaps consent to change their religion and to be like us. We shall then be innocent of bloodshed.'

[1] *'Emak ha-Baka* (the Vale of Weeping), Letteris' edition, pp. 20, *seq.*

As these words found favor in the eyes of the be-
siegers, the governor returned to the town, and called
the Jews together, and proclaimed these words in the
ears of the people, saying: 'Ye know what I have
done unto you from my youth up till this day, how
I have saved you from the hand of the oppressor and
tyrant, as I vowed to you, so that no dog moved his
tongue against any one of you, and not even a shoe-
lace was taken from you. Ye are my witnesses, up
till this day. But now your eyes see that the children
are come to the birth, and there is no strength to
bring forth. A day of trouble and distress, a day of
devastation and desolation, a day of wrath and punishment is this day, and I am not able to withstand the
tyranny of these firebrands that smoke with kindled
anger, lest they should come and smite me, the mother
with the children. Now choose ye for yourselves:
either ye consent to be like us, or ye will be handed
over to them, and they will do unto you as they did
in all the countries through which they passed. Choose
ye for yourselves, that I may be free from sin.' And
all like one man answered, saying: 'It is better that
we should die in the fear of the Lord than that we
should do this thing, and sin against God. Now, our
lord, we are in thy hand, do with us as it seems good
in thine eyes; for evil is determined against us: on
account of us is this great tempest upon you.'

When the governor perceived that he could not
prevail upon them, he acted cunningly, and sent several of the Jews out of the town accompanied by his
servants. Then he commanded that the latter should
return to the town, with their swords stained with
the blood of the beasts of field. And they showed
their swords to the Jews saying: 'See ye what has

been done unto your brethren; in this manner will it be done unto you, if ye do not consent to-day to be like us.' But the Jews all answered like one man, and said: 'We have no portion in your religion, and no inheritance in your god; do unto us as it seems good in your eyes. For the Lord our God is one God; unto Him shall we cleave, Him shall we serve, and by His name shall we swear all the days. We shall not turn aside to the right or to the left from the commandments which Moses the servant of the Lord commanded us.'

Then the governor commanded, and they brought back the Jews whom he had sent outside, and they put them in prison, separately, so that they should not lay hands on one another, as some Jews did in other towns.

There were two women in that town, the name of the one was Gentila, and the name of the other Rebecca. And one of them who was with child bowed herself and brought forth a son, for her pains came upon her. There was nobody with them but a young girl of very beautiful appearance. When she saw that the enemies rose up against them, they took the child, and wrapped him up in clothes, for their mercies grew warm for him, and they threw him down to the ground from the tower in which they were imprisoned. When the enemies saw what they had done, they arose on the following morning, and seized hold upon them, and led them against their will to the high place, and did unto them according to their desire, and there was none to say: 'Halt!' Some were slain with the edge of the sword, others bowed to the idol, after being tortured, on that terrible day, and they turned away from the Lord.

There was a Jew among them, whose name was Shemariah; and the bishop's treasurer said to him: 'Shemariah, Shemariah, fear not; abide with me, and I shall save thee from their hand.' So the man was content to dwell with him, and gave him the money that was found with him. The bishop's treasurer then led away him, his wife, and his three sons, and made them dwell in the forest until the ninth day of Ab, which is the fifth month. Then this base fellow forced him to send to his sons in Spires that they should give him silver pieces or gold pieces. When they sent him some of the money that was found with them, this base fellow took it away, and immediately delivered Shemariah and his family to the hand of the enemy. The inhabitants of the village rejoiced to see him, for they had known him, and consented that he should not change his religion until the following day. So on that day they ate no unclean thing, for they said craftily: 'Let us do to-day according to our custom, but to-morrow about this time we shall become one people.' Whereupon they retired to their room, for they were dejected and fatigued. They closed the door, and spent that night there. And it came to pass in the morning watch that his sleep fled from his eyes, and the man arose before a man could recognize his fellow, and took the knife and slew his children and his wife. He also attempted to cut his throat, but did not succeed, for giddiness took hold of him; he swooned, but did not die.

As soon as the morning was light, the enemies arose against him, and when they saw what he had done, they were exceedingly astounded at him, and said unto him: 'Why hast thou committed such a

XLV. MOSES HAYYIM LUZZATTO

[Italian poet and mystic. He was born at Padua in 1707, and died at Acre in 1747. He was very versatile, and wrote some poetic compositions as well as ethical and mystical treatises. As a poet he chiefly distinguished himself in the allegorical drama which was the fashion of the day. He had a vivid imagination, and his style is vigorous and charming. He also wrote on the methodology of the Talmud. His most popular book is the ethical treatise *Mesillat Yesharim* (Path of the Upright).]

Dialogue Between Understanding and Uprightness [1]

Understanding: O Uprightness, beloved of my soul, let thy heart take courage; like a girdle gird on strength! For when assistance seems very far away, relief comes suddenly to us. When in the blazing heat, in summer drought, the sky is covered with thick darkness of the clouds, whose thunder's roaring makes the earth beneath to quake; when lightning flashes like an arrow; when the wind rends the mounts, as though they were earthen pitchers; when at the sound of the abundance of rain, all ears grow deaf; then the beasts of the forest all together take refuge, and all the young doves flee unto the clefts of rocks. But in a moment, with the radiance of its light, the sun shines forth, and breaks through, and dispels all clouds and darkness, so that the storm is then as though it had not been. Thus likewise He, who rules the world with might, causes relief from

[1] *La-Yesharim Tehillah* (Praise to the Upright), Act II, Scene I. An allegorical drama written mostly in blank verse. As a rule the lines are of ten syllables, but now and then there are lines of six syllables. Each line ends with a word whose accent is on the penult.

trouble to spring forth within a moment unto the contrite.

Uprightness: O Understanding, O joy of my heart, thy comforting has surely enlarged my heart. For now it seems as though from the words of thy mouth I behold an opening for my hope. But be so kind, if thou hast good tidings, withhold it not from me.

Understanding: Would that I had good tidings! I would not hide it. Howbeit, I hope to bring it to thee, though not now. For the worker of righteousness shall not forever fail, nor shall the hope of the perfect perish forever. Though Arrogance now rises high, reaches to the clouds, and rides prosperously on the high places of the earth; he is strong and firmly rooted, waxes mighty in his strength; he abstains not from all his lusts, and sees no trouble, neither does he know affliction's cords; but he will be brought down unto the nether-world, and there shall his pride of heart be humbled; instead of haughtiness he will clothe himself with disgrace like a garment; instead of glory, he shall take shame for ever. But thou, the fruit of thy faithfulness shalt thou find in due time; the end of all the troubles of thy soul shalt thou behold, and be for ever satisfied. And when relief comes, thou wilt be thankful for thy affliction; for sorrows which are past and gone are even as great joys esteemed on the day of bliss; for the recollection of them increases our gladness.

Uprightness: Fain would I (if I could muster strength) endure bravely my bitter lot, according to my wish, O Understanding; but it is hard for me, whenever mine eyes see the two stones of stumbling, Deceit and Folly, who take counsel together to be as pricks to me and cause me grief of soul. For noisily

Folly shouts on the street; she treads on all the highest places of the town with impudent countenance;
she knows no fear, and knows no shame; she breaks
all covenants, annuls all laws; there is no faithfulness
in her; falsehood is her right hand; her merchandise
is violence, perjury, and treachery. She is a sister to
all evil and a mother to all sin; but all the sons of
prudence she oppresses unto death; she sits and speaks
against them, and slanders them amidst bowls of
wine; her inner thoughts are for evil against
them; if she were able, she would devour them as a
fish, or would bite them like an ass, and break
their bones. And likewise is Deceit; for with the
flattering of his mouth he hunts for souls as for a
bird, and he feeds the dolt and fool with poison and
death covered with honey; he bites when he kisses,
and when his hands pretend to cure he bruises; he
does according to all his desire, and yet succeeds.

Understanding: Indeed, it is but the illusion of our
eyes, for they are eyes of flesh, and, therefore, they
confound truth with falsehood. They change darkness into light, and light into darkness. Now, if
in matters that they can perceive, they err at every
occasion and chance, how greatly must they err in
matters hidden and concealed from them! Look at
the end of an oar put in the water: Lo, it appears to
thee twisted and crooked, although thou knowest in
thy heart that in reality it is straight. Sheshai and
Talmai [2] appear like ants, when reflected in a concave
mirror; but in a convex mirror the effect is reversed.
Consider now our spirit, which is like the sea cease-
lessly agitated by the conflicts with the wind: its billows surge wildly, and are tossed about from place to

[2] Names of giants; comp. Numbers 13.22.

place; even so our spirit is never free from grief.
And as our sorrows change the moods of our spirit, so
are our senses changed from time to time: We only
see what we desire; our ears only hear what we long
for, or that which our imagination conceives. If we
would have seen this world with clear eyes but once,
then could we have beheld these our enemies together
so afflicted, stricken, and distressed, that we would
have said: 'Enough! we have had our fill of vengeance!' Lo, as thine eyes see them all filled with
bliss, and satisfied with ease, so truly are their feet
entangled in the net, where they are held since long,
and whence they will not escape; their steps take hold
on the depth of the nether-world; as soon as their feet
slip, they will have no power to rise there again. Now
take thou courage, gird on strength! I shall go now
and look about; if there is aught I hear, I shall return,
and tell thee; for the present rest thou still, and direct the meditations of thy heart and all thy thoughts
according to thy wisdom. Lo, there is no bravery
like the bravery of a man who conquers his strong
passions and rules over his spirit; only the heart that
keeps vexation far away rests and reposes.

XLVI. NAPHTALI HIRZ (HARTWIG) WESSELY

[Educationalist and poet. He was born at Hamburg in 1725, and died in 1805. Although he lacked poetic imagination, his purely biblical style gained for him a great reputation, and he exerted unusual influence on his contemporaries and on subsequent writers. In a certain sense he may be regarded as the father of the modern Hebrew renaissance. He was also the author of a commentary on some books of the Bible, and was an enthusiastic follower of Moses Mendelssohn. His masterpiece is the epic poem entitled *Shire Tif'eret* (Songs of Glory), describing the exodus.]

Moses Prepares the People for the Divine Revelation [1]

Filled with divine rejoicing and words of pleasantness, Moses came down from the mountain unto the people that waited for him. He declared to them the words of their God and said: 'I heard from God's mouth more bliss than ever I hoped for; He will create for you that which has never been since His hands fashioned the earth, O house of Jacob, hark and stand aghast! The voice of the living God from heaven shall ye hear speaking unto you. The laws which ye are to keep shall ye learn now from God's mouth, not from an interpreter. Howbeit, that ye may know that He raised me for His prophet, ye shall behold me bring word between you and God. And seeing that I am esteemed by Him a faithful prophet, ye shall believe me, too, when I enjoin you in His name, that I heard all the commandments from the mouth of God.'

[1] *Shire Tif'eret,* part of canto XVII.

Moses' words were sweeter unto the congregation than melodious strains upon a pleasant harp and psaltery. With joyful voice responded they: ' It is more than we have hoped! Ears that were wont to hear the oppressor's voice, the voice of fear, shall now hear the utterances of the Living God! No people, since there was a nation until now, has ever heard such words! Great is this glory. Now, if God performs all these wonders for the sake of man's soul, so that it may be saved, shall we not turn away from evil, and depart from sin, so that we may deliver our souls from seeing the pit? Our lot is happy if we shall hear these laws from God's mouth; if He speaks, who would be rebellious and would not fear Him? O master, not because there is no faithfulness in us, did we ask thee to let us hear the voice of God. Far be this thought from us! for thou art faithful unto us; we shall obey the law of thy mouth, as though we heard it from God. But thou hast aroused in us the love of God; when thou hast said that God desired to speak with us, our soul has fainted and longed to hear His voice. For we love our Lord and His holy words dearly, so that we may declare to our children that shall be born that from the mouth of our God we heard the laws. We shall tell them, too, of thy greatness and the splendor of thy majesty, how thou stoodest between God and between us, so that all generations shall believe in thee like us. Having been told by their fathers, by six hundred thousand men, that thou art truth and that thy words are truth, they shall not hearken unto prophets that teach lies, and unto strangers.'

These words of the people, too, gladdened Moses' heart; he went up the mountain to bring back word to Him who sent him, and told Him all the words spoken

by the people; and he said: 'Thy people would exult
to hear the majesty of Thy voice; their soul faints and
longs to see Thy glory and Thy might. I pray Thee,
honor and cheer them with the light of Thy countenance; and I, Thy servant, shall make them hear Thy
holy words, as Thou commandest, so that they shall
also believe in me.'

To these words of the man of faithful spirit God
replied: 'I shall do according to thy words: I grant
the wishes of the meek. Their ear shall hear a mighty
voice like which no ear has heard, so that they may
know that the voice of God is wonderful. Yea, a
benign and graceful spirit shall I pour upon them,
so that they may be strengthened, if their heart fails
through fear. In order that My fear should be before them all their days, that they should dread My
majesty, and tremble through their fear, this very
mountain shall be clothed with terror and with dread;
he who sees it shall fear, his heart shall melt, his
hands shall drop; so that My people see that, though
I am a God of plenteous mercy, a pestilence goes before
Me, a fiery bolt is at My feet, and a fire not kindled
by man devours him that contemns My words; so that
they may fear Me always, and never sin. But thou alone
shalt know no fear, for great is thy strength. Thou
shalt walk securely between fire-brands and flames
of fire, for I set on thee a splendor which no other
mortal has. And therefore if thou seest that mighty
men bow themselves, speak comfortably unto them,
and say to them: "Fear not;" I show them but the
lot of the presumptuous and the portion of the wicked;
but I love them that love Me; the perfect shall inherit
good: I shall support their lot, and I alone am their
portion; they that honor Me have peace, securely dwells

he who obeys Me. Great shall be that day, there never
has been one like it! They should therefore prepare
their hearts, My chosen ones shall be sanctified. Go
to the people, and prepare · their hearts with thy
words; teach them to-day My fear, and sanctify them
to-morrow; they shall wash their garments, and bathe
their flesh; and they shall be ready on the third day
in the morning. For on the third day (that is the
very day on which I chose to give to them the Law of
truth and righteous ordinances) shall God come down
from His throne in heaven upon this mount, yea,
on this mount Sinai in holiness. A glorious appearance which no eye has yet beheld shall be upon
its top, which I shall show to the people. Although I
am a God that hide Myself, no mortal eye sees Me,
the splendor is the sign that I dwell there and that
there is the hiding of My power. And as before the
arrival of the day on which I speak to them, all the
people shall for two days sanctify themselves, so likewise shall the mountain, before I shine forth from it,
be prepared and sanctified for two days: allow not
the feet of man or beast to come on it; set bounds
about the mountain, the boundary being all around,
so that people do not cross the bounds which thou hast
set. And say to them: "Take heed that ye ascend
not the mount; nor shall ye touch it: he that touches
it shall surely die." And even they that pursue the
transgressor shall not tread on the mount; from afar
shall he be stoned, or arrows shall be shot at, him.
All who go up the mountain, whether man or beast,
shall die; this mount with all that is around it shall
henceforth be holy ground to you, for with My glory
will I adorn it. But when My glory is taken off from
it, I will give a sign: the trumpet's voice shall I

cause to be heard from the top of the mount. Not like the voice of the trumpet which they will hear when I arrive—a terrifying voice, that all wicked hearts may be humbled and fear God their Creator and observe His law—but when My glory ascends, departing from the earth, the trumpet shall be blown in honor and might to My name; and when the trumpet sounds long, they also shall come up to the mount.'

The Lord Baltimore Press
BALTIMORE, MD., U. S. A.

This book may be kept
FOURTEEN DAYS
A fine will be charged for each
day the book is kept overtime.
